FINISHING THE

GREAT COMMISSION

**A CHALLENGE TO THE CHURCH
TO COMPLETE A 2000-YEAR-OLD MANDATE!**

Foreword by
DR. DAVID SHIBLEY

WALE BABATUNDE

Christian Heritage Publication

An Imprint of:
Great Commission Incorporation
7 Enmore Road
South Norwood
London
SE25 5NQ
United Kingdom

Scripture Quotations are taken from:
King James (KJV) Bible © Crown Copyright
New King James (NKJV) Bible © 1982 by Thomas Nelson Inc
New International Version (NIV) Bible
Used by permission. All rights reserved
ISBN: 978-0-9570933-5-5
Cover design: CCD Media Limited
Book Transformation Work (Copy Editing & Proofreading) – Mrs Nana Fosua Babatunde
Printed and bound in the UK by SpiffingCovers
From CCD Limited, UK

CONTENTS

CONTENTS

DEDICATION

I dedicate this book to our Lord and Saviour, Jesus Christ, for giving me what I consider the greatest privilege in my life to serve in the Kingdom of God. He has been faithful all through the years and I am ever so grateful. Jesus, I love you; Jesus, I thank you; Jesus, I bless you for journeying with me all these years.

ACKNOWLEDGEMENTS

As the building of a nation cannot be done overnight and by one man, so also the writing of this book would not have been possible, but for the help, encouragement and inspiration from many - both near and far.

- To Nana Fosua, for her patience, encouragement and first-class editorial work.
- To Kola Sekoni, for his service and partnership in bringing this book to life.
- To Joshua, Grace, Jeremiah and Elisha-Joseph, for their love and encouragement over the years.
- To all the leaders and members of World Harvest Christian Centre, for their support and prayers and also the platform given me to serve God.
- My sincerest appreciation goes to all the Pastors, mentors, lecturers, teachers and

speakers who have impacted and poured into my life for almost 40 years, and without whose input this book would have been impossible. I am convinced that many of the thoughts and views in this book should have been attributed to them if my memory serves me right.

FOREWORD

"There comes a point in our lives as followers of Jesus when we must make some crucial choices. Either we fall victim to the spirit of the age and embrace the cult of self or we live on a higher plane. The godly Francis Xavier challenged the apathetic European students of his day to *"give up your small ambitions and come and preach the Gospel of Christ."*

Now, Pastor Wale Babatunde issues the same challenge to our generation in his timely book, *Finishing the Great Commission*. Passion for Christ's global glory leaps from every page. You will be challenged by his stories, statistics, and biblically-based zeal to find your role in extending the fame of Jesus' name in your neighbourhood and around the world.

Some years back I spent a day at Yale Divinity School researching the original papers of the Student Volunteer Movement and the eminent missionary statesman, John R. Mott. Almost 120 years ago, Mott penned an eloquent plea to fulfil Christ's commission. His book was titled, *The Evangelization of the World in This Generation*. Before the book's publication, he sent manuscript copies to selected people, asking for their comments and suggestions.

One of these manuscripts went to Hudson Taylor in China. Now, all these years later, I was holding in my hands the very letter from Hudson Taylor to John R. Mott, dated 17 May 1900. As I held Taylor's letter, a chill ran down my spine as I sensed a glorious link with these giants of an earlier era. I wondered what Taylor would think of the developments in China today and its brave, vigorous church (much of which dates its roots back to Taylor's missionary work). I mused how John R. Mott, one of the prime movers of student missions in his day, would rejoice in today's new youth missions movement. Then I remembered that Taylor and Mott do, in fact, see it all. They are part of heaven's great cloud of witnesses. Looking again at Hudson Taylor's letter, I read:

"The evangelization of the world depends on the full surrender of every Christian both at home and abroad, so that the Holy Spirit may be unhindered. Appeal to every reader to unhesitatingly take this position."

This is the heart-cry of Pastor Babatunde's book, as well. Full surrender – take this position *now!* Let God take your precious life and use you for His purposes in ways beyond your highest hopes and dreams. You have *"come to the kingdom for such a time as this"* (Esther 4:14).

Finishing the Great Commission is a clarion call to "have done with lesser things." The Church of Jesus Christ has done incalculable good worldwide since our Lord's ascension. However, we have left undone the single mandate he left us: get the Gospel to every person and make disciples of every nation. Wale Babatunde has set the trumpet to his lips that calls us to finish the task. May we live for what matters. And what matters most is the exaltation of the Son of God to the ends of the earth."

David Shibley
Founder and World Representative of Global Advance
USA

ENDORSEMENTS

"For over 25 years, Wale Babatunde has devoted his life and ministry to equip, empower, and mobilise The Church to bring closure to the Great Commission. "Finishing The Great Commission" is an insightful look at The Church's mandate, a convicting progress report on the status of world evangelism, and a practical approach to becoming a part of Christ's Kingdom endeavour. This book will inspire you and your church to engage the unreached peoples of our world and to proclaim the Good News of Salvation to those that have never heard it."

Matt Bennett
President of SpiritLife Ministries International
Director of Graduate Studies at Southwestern Christian University
USA

"Thank God for all who are exhorting us to get serious about finishing The Great Commission and thank God for this exhortation to do so from Wale Babatunde. May God help us take seriously this challenge from Pastor Babatunde and renew our personal commitments to help finish this task. Two thousand years is long enough to have an assignment from Jesus without completing it. Let's get it done. Thanks, Pastor, for this challenge. May God use it for His glory."

James R. Eby
Founder/President, Mission Catalyst International, Inc.
USA

Finishing the Great Commission is an urgent call to the Church of God to mobilise and fulfil God's great mission. The Church is God's redemptive vehicle on the earth. Our message is one of redemption, salvation and hope. It is a message of reconciling a fallen and sinful world back to the original design and intent of God.

The Great Commission is as clear today as it was over 2000 years ago.

Wale Babatunde frames the importance of the Great Commission with clarity and a sense of urgency rarely felt or even preached from the pulpit. He delivers a passionate message that must be heeded and become the driving force of the Church again.

In reading this book, Wale provides you with the blueprint with practical applications needed to heed the call to fulfilling the Great Commission.

This book is necessary for a time such as this as it definitively written to reveal God's heart and passion for a lost and dying world.

Bishop D.A. Lazarus
Visionary and Founder: Siloam
Presiding Bishop: Siloam and Kingdom Builders Network
Diocesan Bishop: United Covenant Churches Of Christ, Africa
South Africa

INTRODUCTION

It is almost inconceivable that after two thousand years, the Church is yet to finish the ONLY assignment the Lord of the Church gave to us. It is even more surprising that in spite of the fact that close to 40% of the world's population is yet to be reached with the Gospel of Jesus Christ, the thought of finishing the Great Commission in our generation is hardly paramount on our agenda.

It seems to me that the Church's attention has been diverted to programmes, projects, and issues that have not been commanded by the Lord of the Harvest.

The message in this book is a wake-up call for the sleeping giant – the Church. No other generation has been so enriched by God, yet does so little for the expansion of the Kingdom.

The harvest is NOW! We can no longer delay! The eternal destinies of billions are in the balance. The Church must only have one priority – SOULS! All our resources - money, workers and time, must be channelled towards taking the Good News to the regions beyond. The whole Church must be mobilized to take the whole Gospel to the whole world!

In order to accomplish this royal assignment, the Church must embrace a simple and sacrificial lifestyle and disposition. We must also channel more prayers and financial resources towards the unsaved, particularly the unreached people groups.

I pray that God, in His mercy, would send to us in this generation a great revival that would birth the greatest missionary movement that the world has seen, to usher in the long-awaited coming of our Lord and Saviour – KING JESUS!

> *Jesus shall reign where'er the sun,*
> *Does his successive journeys run,*
> *His kingdom stretch from shore to shore,*
> *Till moons shall wax and wane no more*
>
> *For Him shall endless prayer be made,*
> *And endless praises crown His head;*
> *His name, like sweet perfume, shall rise*
> *With ev'ry morning sacrifice*
>
> *People and realms of ev'ry tongue*
> *Dwell on His love with sweetest song;*
> *And infant voices shall proclaim*
> *Their early blessings on His name*

Blessings abound where'er He reigns;
The pris'ner leaps, unloosed his chains,
The weary find eternal rest,
And all the sons of want are blest.

Let every creature rise and bring
Peculiar honors to our King;
Angels descend with songs again,
And earth repeat the loud Amen!

- (Isaac Watts, 1719)

CHAPTER 1

THE GREAT COMMISSION

Before Jesus ascended into Heaven roughly about two thousand years ago, he called his disciples, later called Apostles, and entrusted them with just one assignment – To make Him known throughout the world:

- They were to introduce Him to every creature.
- They were to go and share the Good News that the Lamb had been sacrificed; that God had made peace with man, and that He was no longer angry with mankind.
- That after our fall in the Garden of Eden, we can now be reconciled to God.
- That no one ever has to end up in Hell, which was originally prepared for Satan and his fellow angels.
- The disciples of Jesus were to go to every people or ethnic group, share the redemption

story, and disciple them with the message of the Cross.

Why did Jesus Defer the Giving of The Great Commission?

I have often asked myself this question – why did Jesus defer the giving of The Great Commission Mandate to the very last moment before he ascended into Heaven? Was it an oversight or was there a more strategic reason for this?

Quite often, when I'm travelling out of the country, shortly before the plane takes off, I suddenly remember some important tasks that my administrator or some of my associates need to attend to before I return. On such occasions, I get on my phone and give them one or two instructions. In comparison, could it have been that Jesus experienced the same thing? Was it that Jesus forgot that he had a very important assignment for His disciples, but suddenly remembered at the point of departure or ascension? Certainly not! I am definitely of the opinion that He delayed the giving of this mandate because of its strategic importance.

I reckon that if Jesus had given this task at the beginning, or even somewhere in the middle of His ministerial career, the disciples would have lost its significance.

A Man's Will

There are many things a man or woman will do in their lifetime; there are many thoughts, wishes, contracts or instructions that we will write or express. However, none are as significant as a person's will. A will is a person's last statement, which represents his or her wishes. A will is a sacred and important document. Usually, the executors are bound under oath to follow the wishes of the testator to the letter!

It is often said that the last words of a dying man are very significant. I have often asked friends and families who have lost loved ones – father, mother, brother, sister, uncle, aunt, or someone very close to them, how important the last words or wishes of the deceased were to them. Without exception, the responses have always been the same – very important! They cherished those words or instructions and made sure that they carried out the last wishes of the deceased as instructed. It is in this light that Jesus' last wishes or instructions must be understood and appreciated. It is not The Great Omission, but The Great Commission.

The Great Commission
Have you ever wondered why the parting words of Jesus to His disciples is referred to as The Great Commission? I believe it is simply because no work, assignment, project or commission that the Church could embark on, however lofty they may be, could be more important than the commission to win and disciple souls.

The Great Suggestion or Command?
"And he said unto them, Go ye into all the world, and preach the Gospel to every creature." – Mark 16:15 (KJV)

23

"Go ye therefore, and teach all nations, baptizing them in the name of the Father, and of the Son, and of the Holy Ghost" – *Matthew 28:19 (KJV)*

Quite frequently, most of us receive advice or suggestions from friends, family, colleagues, mentors or even our spiritual guides. Our finance or investment mentors will for example, suggest that we save regularly and invest wisely if we are going to enjoy financial independence. Regularly, I advise my children to take their education seriously, be prudent with their finances and to relate only with serious and godly friends and peers. As a boy growing up under my father's guide, I was always advised on the importance of hard-work, educational excellence, and character development.

In view of all this, however, one thing is clear about suggestions or advice – you are not obliged to comply with them.

NOTE THIS! - The Great Commission is a command, and not a suggestion or advice.

When Jesus gave us the marching order, He wasn't telling us as His followers that it was a nice thing to share our Faith and make disciples of all nations; it was a command! We have no option when it comes to the issue of carrying out The Great Commission. It wasn't something we could do when we like or when it is convenient. As our commander in chief, He was ordering us to execute His bidding.

I have always wondered how soldiers would obey the orders of their superiors even when they know it could cost them their lives; all for king and country. While writing, I was privileged to share fellowship with a family friend who has served in the U.S. Army for over two decades. I got into a conversation with him regarding what a command meant to him as a military officer. In his words, "when you are given a command, the next thing is to execute it!" According to Him, every command must be taken literally. For example, if you are given a command to go and kill your father, there are no sentiments; the order must be fully obeyed. Failing this, there would be severe consequences.

The issue that confronted me during my discussion with my friend was "Is this how we view Jesus' last command to the Church?" Do we take seriously our commander's charge? Do we not have a lot to learn from the world's system? Could it be one of the reasons why Jesus declared that *"...the children of this world are wiser in their generation?" (Luke 16:8)*

The God of the Bible, we must always remind ourselves, demands complete obedience to His commands, instructions and biddings. It is, therefore, no surprise that the first king of Israel was sanctioned and later replaced because he didn't fully comply with divine commands. The list is endless in the Bible of individuals who were reprimanded for not obeying God's instructions.

In order to function effectively in the military, the first thing that must happen is to change the mindset of every civilian to a soldier's. If there was something that is much needed in this age, it is the transformation of our minds. Most Believers today function as civilians, even though they have been conscripted into the Lord's Army.

"And be not conformed to this world: but be ye transformed by the renewing of your mind..." – Romans 12:2 (KJV)

Could it be that it was because Paul, the Apostle, saw the fulfilment of The Great Commission as a command, that he placed a curse on himself if he didn't preach the Gospel? (1 Corinthians 9:16)

Practical Applications for Finishing the Great Commission

1. In your own words, what do you believe the Great Commission entails?
2. The Great Commission was Jesus' last will to the Church. How well are you and your local fellowship obeying Jesus' will or testament?
3. Do you personally take the Great Commission as a command or a suggestion?

CHAPTER 2

OUR MARCHING ORDER!

Jesus gave the Church the marching order to take the Good News to the ends of the earth over two thousand years ago! I have always wondered why it has taken the Church this long to take the Gospel to just a little over half of the world's population while the Coca-Cola brand is virtually in every nook and cranny of the globe.

I often hear Believers and Christian leaders remark that they are waiting on God to send them to the nations. Sometimes I am taken aback as to what "waiting on God" means! Is it not just another spiritual cliché? I thought He already gave us the marching order over two thousand years ago! While most of us claim we are waiting on God, I think God is actually the one waiting on the Church to rise up from our slumber and obey the marching order.

For any avoidance of doubt regarding Jesus' mandate to the Church, the New Testament records at least five different passages where Christ gave us the marching order. Let's consider them:

"And Jesus came and spoke unto them, saying, All power is given unto me in Heaven and in earth. Go ye therefore, and teach all nations, baptizing them in the name of the Father, and of the Son, and of the Holy Ghost: Teaching them to observe all things whatsoever I have commanded you: and, lo, I am with you alway, even unto the end of the world. Amen" - Matthew 28:18-20 (KJV)

Again in Mark 16:15-18 *"And he said to them, Go ye into all the world, and preach the Gospel to every creature. He that believeth and is baptized shall be saved; but he that believeth not shall be damned. And these signs shall follow them that believe; In my name shall they cast out devils; they shall speak with new tongues; They shall take up serpents; and if they drink any deadly thing, it shall not hurt them; they shall lay hands on the sick, and they shall recover."* (KJV)

The Lukan version is from chapter 24, verses 46 to 48, *"And said unto them, thus it is written, and thus it behoved Christ to suffer, and to rise from the dead the third day: And that repentance and remission of sins should be preached in his name among all nations, beginning at Jerusalem. And ye are witnesses of these things."* (KJV)

The fourth passage in the New Testament of Jesus giving the Church the marching order is in John chapter

20, verse 21, *"Then said Jesus to them again, Peace be unto you: as my father hath sent me, even so send I you." (KJV)*

The fifth and final Scripture is in Acts 1, verse 8, *"But ye shall receive power, after that the Holy Ghost is come upon you: and ye shall be witnesses unto me both in Jerusalem, and in all Judea, and in Samaria, and unto the uttermost part of the earth."* (KJV). No serious student of the New Testament would fail to see how important Jesus' instruction was to the Church.

The Promise of Supernatural Power & Enduement

When God sent Moses to Pharaoh in Egypt to deliver the children of Israel, it was not without signs and wonders. Moses had to validate his mission and ministry by the supernatural workings of God.

Jesus Himself declared that without seeing and experiencing the supernatural, the people would not believe. *"Then said Jesus unto him, Except ye see signs and wonders, ye would not believe"* - John 4:48 (KJV).

Paul, the Apostle, himself declared what manner of ministry he exerted! It wasn't just philosophical speculations and mere rhetorics. His ministry was accompanied by the supernatural. To the Corinthian Church, he declared,

"And I, brethren, when I came to you, came not with excellency of speech or of wisdom, declaring unto you the testimony of God. For I determined not to know any thing among you, save Jesus Christ, and him crucified. And I was with you in weakness, and in fear, and in much

trembling. And my speech and my preaching was not with enticing words of man's wisdom, but in demonstration of the Spirit and of power: That your faith should not stand in the wisdom of men, but in the power of God." - 1 Corinthians 2:1-5 (KJV)

Therefore, when Jesus gave the Church the marching order, it was backed by the promise of power and supernatural presence. Let's consider the following passages:

1. **Matthew 28:20** - *"...Lo I am with you alway, even unto the end of the world. Amen."* (KJV). This speaks of the presence of the Holy Spirit.

2. **Mark 16:20** - *"...The Lord working with them, and confirming the word with signs following. Amen". (KJV)*

3. **Luke 24:49** - *"And behold, I send the promise of my Father upon you: but tarry ye in the city of Jerusalem, until you are endued with power from on high". (KJV)*

4. **John 20:22** - *"And when he had said this, he breathed on them, and saith unto them, Receive ye the Holy Ghost". (KJV)*

5. **Acts 1:4-5** - *"And, being assembled together with them, commanded them that they should not depart from Jerusalem, but wait for the promise of the Father, which, saith he, ye have heard of me. For John truly baptized with water; but ye shall be baptized with the Holy Ghost not many days hence!" (KJV)*

What our Assignment Entails

Anytime the British military is sent on an overseas mission, their commanding officer always gives them detailed instructions. Jesus didn't leave the Church in doubt regarding what our mission entails. Let's consider a few things we are meant to do as we obey the marching order. There are 3 verbs (action words) in the Great Commission that we are meant to obey;

1. **Go** - We are always meant to be on the Go. Christians and Churches that are stationary are being disobedient! Too many General Overseers are just stagnant with this mandate. Every General Overseer, and indeed every Believer, must be on the GO!

2. **Baptise** - I have often heard debates as to whether or not it is compulsory for repentant sinners to be baptised. My response is yes! The Master commanded us to baptise people. I'm sure the question some of you might ask is - could someone make Heaven without baptism? Yes! Let's refer to the thief at the right-hand side of Jesus when nailed to the Cross. Jesus declared to him, "...Verily I say unto thee, To day shalt thou be with me in paradise." – Luke 23:43 (KJV). No baptism, therefore, occurred.

3. **Teach** - Teaching is central to the Great Commission. As a result, if we are going to be faithful in fulfilling this mandate, we must recover the teaching ministry, which I believe

31

has been largely put behind the burner.

4. **Discipleship** - The Commission tasks us to disciple primarily the nations or ethnic groups (Matt 28:19 – NIV) with kingdom values and ways of life. This, does not in any way rule out discipling individuals, as opposed to us making converts.

5. **Church Planting** – I believe, by implication, we are to plant churches or fellowships as we preach the Gospel and people turn-around to receive Christ. What other ways are we to disciple people if not in the company of other Believers? I don't believe there's only one expression of church. We must be able to express church in different forms as occasions demand. Could church planting be one of the keys to completing the Great Commission? I believe so! One of the foremost missiologists of the 20th century, Peter Wagner, declares in his book, "Church Planting for Greater Harvest", that church planting is the most effective evangelistic method under Heaven.

Practical Applications for Finishing the Great Commission

1. Can you write the 5 scriptures in the New Testament where Jesus gave the Church the marching order?

2. Can you identify the verbs (action words) in the

Great Commission?

3. How important is a marching order to a soldier? Compared with the military, how do you think Christians are faring?

CHAPTER 3

FINISHING THE GREAT COMMISSION

One thing that I would like to make very clear throughout this book is that, once Christ entrusted the Church with the Great Commission, He expected us to finish the assignment. Unfortunately, I'm not sure that most Believers and even Church leaders see this as a priority! I have read several books in my lifetime, attended many church services, seminars, anniversaries and conventions, yet completing the Great Commission hardly comes into focus.

In the Olivet discourse, Jesus highlighted the various signs that would characterise the whole course of the last days, which would intensify as the end draws nearer. The disciples asked Jesus three interesting questions - *"Tell us, when shall these things be? and what shall be the sign of thy coming, and of the end of the world?" - Matthew 24:3 (KJV)*

According to prophecy experts, these signs deal with the destruction of Jerusalem, the rapture of the Church, and the end of the Age. The signs include:

1. Deception
2. Wars and Rumours of war
3. Nations (Ethnic groups) rising against nations, and kingdoms against kingdoms
4. Natural disasters - earthquakes, famines, pestilence and other disasters
5. The Persecution of True Believers
6. Increase in lawlessness, leading to spiritual apathy
7. Mass offences and betrayal
8. The preaching of the Gospel

One thing is clear to me from Jesus' Olivet discussions and my prophetic understanding - the preaching of the Gospel would be the final sign that will precede the golden-age. The End would only come after the "Gospel of the Kingdom" has been adequately preached in all the world as a witness. The question that the disciples asked was *"what shall be the sign of thy coming...?" (Matt. 24:3)*. To this question, Jesus responded in Matthew 24:14 – *"And this gospel of the kingdom shall be preached in all the world for a witness unto all nations; and then shall the end come." (KJV)*

When Christ commissioned us to take the Gospel to the ends of the earth, He expected us to finish the assignment by taking the Good News to every nation, people and individual.

Have you not realised that our God never begins anything that He would not finish? This is why He is called the Alpha and Omega; the First and the Last; the Author and the Finisher!

Jesus was a Finisher
If there was something that engrossed the mind of our Saviour, it was the passion to finish what He came to the earth to do. He was ever so focused, ignored frivolities and was very conscious of His destiny.

At least twice, the Messiah declared unequivocally that He had completed His assignment on earth.

"I have glorified thee on the earth: I have finished the work which thou gavest me to do."
- John 17:4 (KJV)

Again, on the Cross:

"When Jesus therefore had received the vinegar, he said, It is finished: and he bowed his head, and gave up the ghost." – John 19:30 (KJV)

Paul - A Great Finisher
Paul, the greatest of all the Apostles, like his master, was consumed with finishing his assignment on earth.

In Acts 20:17-24, when he was giving his valedictory speech to the Ephesian elders, he recounted amongst many other things, the myriad of challenges, trials and afflictions that he had to endure in the discharge of his duties. He remarked that none of those things really bothered or concerned him, except for one thing - Finishing the Ministry that he had received from the Lord.

> *"But none of these things move me, neither count I my life dear unto myself, so that I might finish my course with joy, and the ministry, which I have received of the Lord Jesus, to testify the gospel of the grace of God." - Act 20:24 (KJV)*

Towards the end of his life, writing what many considered to be his last epistle, Paul seems to mark his own examination papers;

> *"For I am now ready to be offered, and the time of my departure is at hand. I have fought a good fight, I have finished my course, I have kept the faith." - 2 Timothy 4:6-7 (KJV)*

Does it bother you whether or not you finish the assignment that God has appointed to you?!

Are we, who could undoubtedly be considered as the most privileged generation, with everything at our disposal, concerned at all with concluding the Great Commission in our generation? Does it ever preoccupy our minds at all? Does it come up in our Pastors' fraternity or are we just concerned about building our own empires?

The End – A Divine Factor

For many years, I had always thought that the return of Jesus to take away his bride was simply a divine factor. That is, God in His sovereignty would just decide whenever He deems fit. After all, Jesus had declared that *"But of that day and hour knoweth no man, no, not the angels of Heaven, but my Father only"* - Matthew 24:36 (KJV)

However after reading Matthew 24:3 & 14, I came to the conclusion that the End would not just be a divine factor, but it would hinge on how well we have done with our Commission to take the Gospel to the ends of the earth as a witness. To buttress my point, Peter seems to corroborate this idea:

> *"Looking for and hasting unto the coming of the day of God, wherein the Heavens being on fire shall be dissolved, and the elements shall melt with fervent heat?"* - 2 Peter 3:12 (KJV)

> *"Looking for and earnestly desiring the coming of..."* (ASV)

> *"Expecting and helping to hasten the coming of..."* (WEY)

> *"Look eagerly for the coming of the day of God and work to hasten it on..."* (WEB)

From all the various translations, Peter seems to be saying that Believers could hasten Christ's return. Conversely, by our lukewarm, lethargic and indifferent attitude to the completion of the Great Commission, we could delay Christ's coming!

Practical Application for Finishing the Great Commission
1. Why do you think it is vital for us to take the Gospel to all the unreached people groups? (see Matthew 24:14)
2. Do you believe the consummation of all things is a divine prerogative or is it linked to what the Church does?
3. Mention 4 things Believers/ the Church can do to hasten the second coming.

CHAPTER 4
THE PRIORITY OF THE GOSPEL

"The mission of the Church is missions." –
Oswald J. Smith

"Only as the Church fulfils her missionary
obligation does she justify her existence." -
Oswald J. Smith

"Our God of Grace often gives us a second
chance, but there is no second chance to harvest
a ripe crop.." – Kurt Von Schleicher

"The Lord did not tell us to build beautiful churches
but to evangelise the world." – Oswald J. Smith

"And the gospel must first be published among
all nations." - Mark 13:10 (KJV)

If we are going to finish the Great Commission in our generation, one thing we must recover is the priority of the Gospel or soul winning. The Church must be clear about one thing – our primary purpose is to win souls. We must understand that soul winning and world evangelisation are our number one priority.

In his discourse of the signs of the age, Mark adds something that we often neglect – "the Gospel must first be preached or published". I would love to highlight the word "FIRST". What does the word mean? It means before anything else or of greater importance. When a student comes first in his class, it means he is ahead of everyone; the same with an athlete. In the same vein, the leader of our nation in Britain is called the Prime Minister; Primus inter pares. This person is therefore first among equals.

What lessons could we learn from all these? We are not only commissioned to preach the Gospel; it must always be our number one priority. When I was sitting my secondary school leaving examinations, I studied Economics as a subject and one of the primary principles we were taught was the "Scale of Preference". This principle stipulates that every individual has a list of needs that they would always want to meet, which may be written or unwritten. At the top of this list would be the most pressing need, with the less pressing needs following suit in that hierarchy. Based on the level of importance of one's needs, they would be placed either at the top or bottom of the scale. For example, as a family man, my scale of preference may look like this:

Did you notice that giving to God and paying my mortgage and bills are high or top priorities while going on holidays is important but not a pressing need? In the same vein, every church ministry, Minister of the Gospel and Believer must have a scale of preference and be conscious of the fact that our number one priority is to preach the Gospel and win souls. This seems very logical, however, the reality is that most churches and Church leaders don't make soul winning and spreading the Gospel to the ends of the earth a number one priority.

There are so many things that the Church is involved in today that are really lofty and many of them, laudable and beneficial to the society, but these should in no way replace our number one priority. I commend Christian ministries and Ministers who are fully involved in education, healthcare, social justice and all the spheres of the society, however, I still want to argue that this is not our primary assignment.

Over the years, there has been a lot of debate as to whether the Church should solely be involved with spiritual business and totally neglect practical needs. I believe we should do both – however, our involvement in the Social Gospel must have as its aim, converting souls into the Kingdom.

I have read of and seen many Christian organisations that are doing a great job, ministering to the social and practical needs of the society, but would never share the Good News with people. Sometimes, we can be so engrossed and distracted by good works that we ignore proclamation evangelism.

What does it mean for us to recover our priority of the Gospel? It means in prayers, budgets, travels and programmes, soul winning must be number ONE. It means one of the key ways to measure our success or effectiveness is how many souls are being saved into the kingdom; how many lives are being inspired and equipped to take the Good News to the unreached. It is only when we place soul winning as our priority that we can even think of finishing the Great Commission.

As a Pastor and a Missionary, I don't get the sense at all that soul winning and finishing the Great Commission is a priority in many places I visit. I believe the Church needs a serious awakening. The sleeping giant must be woken up!

Practical Application for Finishing the Great Commission

1. What does it mean for something to be a priority?
2. In your estimation, do you believe soul winning and the Great Commission is a priority in our churches? Give reasons to back your claim.
3. *"The mission of the church is Missions" – Oswald J. Smith*. What does this mean to you?

CHAPTER 5
THE OUTWARD-LOOKING CHURCH

"Lost people matter to God, and so they must matter to us."– Keith Wright

"Let my heart be broken by the things that break God's heart." – Bob Pierce

"I thought it reasonable that I should seek the work where the work was the most abundant, and the workers fewest." - James Gilmour

"If you take missions out of the Bible, you won't have anything left but the covers." - Nina Gunter

At this juncture in human history, when Biblical prophecies regarding the last days are being fulfilled before our very eyes, where should the attention of the Church be? If we are going to bring back the King in our generation, where should the bulk of our finances be diverted to? Where should we direct most of our "foot soldiers" or workforce? Where should we be channelling our prayers? What should be the focus of most of our seminars, conventions, retreats and media drive?

Jesus, in three related parables, gives us a clue as to where our attention should be focused:

The Parable of the Lost Sheep

"Then drew near unto him all the publicans and sinners for to hear him. And the Pharisees and scribes murmured, saying, This man receiveth sinners, and eateth with them. And he spake this parable unto them, saying, What man of you, having an hundred sheep, if he lose one of them, doth not leave the ninety and nine in the wilderness, and go after that which is lost, until he find it? And when he hath found it, he layeth it on his shoulders, rejoicing. And when he cometh home, he calleth together his friends and neighbours, saying unto them, Rejoice with me; for I have found my sheep which was lost. I say unto you, that likewise joy shall be in Heaven over one sinner that repenteth, more than over ninety and nine just persons, which need no repentance." - Luke 15:1–7 (KJV)

Notice with me that the focus of this parable was on the lost sheep! Even though the Shepherd had ninety-nine other sheep that were safe, he still went after just one that had strayed. I wonder if the Church has not lost the value of the "one soul". Would a modern-day Pastor leave his ninety-nine saved and sanctified members and go after that one lost soul? Would our church fellowships leave those that are saved and go after the ones who are in the unreached people groups and share the love of God? Jesus declared that there would be joy over one sinner that repents, more than over the ninety-nine just persons. Again, we must not lose the focus of the Shepherd. His energy, attention and resources were directed to the one that was lost. This is what I refer to as "the outward-looking church" - the church that is forever looking outside of the confines of the saved.

The Lost Piece of Silver

> *"Either what woman having ten pieces of silver, if she lose one piece, doth not light a candle, and sweep the house, and seek diligently till she find it? And when she hath found it, she calleth her friends and her neighbours together, saying, Rejoice with me; for I have found the piece which I had lost. Likewise, I say unto you, there is joy in the presence of the angels of God over one sinner that repenteth."*
> *- Luke 15:8–10 (KJV)*

In the second parable, a woman has 10 pieces of silver, loses one, and thereafter diligently searches for it. Notice her efforts in recovering the lost coin; she lit a candle, swept the whole house, and diligently searched - all because she was after just one coin. This is the kind of focus, tenacity and determination that Christ wants us to expend when it comes to sinners and the unreached people. Our primary focus should always be outside the safe four walls of our ministries. We must target and reach the lost at all cost!

The Lost Son

> "And he said, A certain man had two sons: And the younger of them said to his father, Father, give me the portion of goods that falleth to me. And he divided unto them his living. And not many days after the younger son gathered all together, and took his journey into a far country, and there wasted his substance with riotous living. And when he had spent all, there arose a mighty famine in that land; and he began to be in want. And he went and joined himself to a citizen of that country; and he sent him into his fields to feed swine. And he would fain have filled his belly with the husks that the swine did eat: and no man gave unto him. And when he came to himself, he said, How many hired servants of my father's have bread enough and to spare, and I perish with hunger! I would arise and go

to my father, and would say unto him, Father, I have sinned against Heaven, and before thee, And am no more worthy to be called thy son: make me as one of thy hired servants. And he arose, and came to his father. But when he was yet a great way off, his father saw him, and had compassion, and ran, and fell on his neck, and kissed him. And the son said unto him, Father, I have sinned against Heaven, and in thy sight, and am no more worthy to be called thy son. But the father said to his servants, Bring forth the best robe, and put it on him; and put a ring on his hand, and shoes on his feet: And bring hither the fatted calf, and kill it; and let us eat, and be merry: For this my son was dead, and is alive again; he was lost, and is found. And they began to be merry." - Luke 15: 11–24 (KJV)

Like the two preceding parables, the last one emphasises the importance of placing priority on the lost. Look at the father's reaction to his son's repentance:

- His father ran to him
- He had compassion on him
- Fell on his neck
- Kissed him
- Changed his robe
- Put a ring on him
- Wore shoes on his feet; and
- Threw a lavish party.

The moral of the three parables is that the Church must place a high premium on what Heaven places a premium on - the lost! In Luke 19:10, Jesus declared his mission and purpose; *"For the Son of man is come to seek and to save that which was lost" (KJV)*. If this was Jesus' mission, should the Church do any less?

The Two Kinds of Lost People

Generally speaking, there are two kinds of people who are lost - who we must give our utmost priority to:

1. <u>Heard the Gospel but still lost</u> - There is a large percentage of people today who fall into this category. They are lost, not because they have not been presented with an opportunity to be saved. They are lost because they have not made a decision to accept Christ as their Lord and personal Saviour. For example, Paul presented the Gospel to Felix and what was his response?

   "...Go thy way for this time; when I have a convenient season, I would call for thee." – Acts 24:25 (KJV)

   It is estimated that at least 40% of the world's population have been presented with the Gospel, but they are yet to make a decision.

2. <u>Lost and never heard the Gospel</u> - Conservative estimates tell us that about 30% of the world's population have not heard the Gospel once. These people are mainly located in the "10/40 Window" and mostly fall under the unreached people groups:

- These people don't have a single living church:
- They are mostly without the Bible in their mother tongue.
- They also don't have a single Missionary among them.

I am of the opinion that it is among these precious people that the we as a Church, must place our primary focus if we are going to finish the Great Commission.

Practical Application for Finishing the Great Commission

1. What does it mean for a church to be outward-looking?
2. Jesus shared three parables to demonstrate that Christians must be outward looking. Can you identify these?
3. There are two categories of lost people. Who are they?
4. What are the negative consequences of an inward-looking ministry?

CHAPTER 6
THE REGIONS BEYOND

"Yea, so have I strived to preach the gospel, not where Christ was named, lest I should build upon another man's foundation:" – Romans 15:20 (KJV)

"As long as there are millions destitute of the Word of God and knowledge of Jesus Christ, it would be impossible for me to devote time and energy to those who have both." – J.L. Ewen

"No one has the right to hear the Gospel twice, while there remains someone who has not heard it once." - Oswald J. Smith

"I have but one candle of life to burn, and I would rather burn it out in a land filled with

darkness than in a land flooded with light." -
John Keith Falconer

In order to be successful in any venture, an individual or corporate organisation must have at least two things:

The first is a clear vision which speaks of where one is heading. What is to be accomplished?

The second is a well-thought-out strategy. If vision deals with "What", strategy deals with "How". If our goal or vision is to reach one thousand souls this year, the strategy would be how we intend to achieve that.

Reading the epistle of Paul, I am totally convinced that Paul had the goal of reaching his world with the Gospel. In fact, it could be said that this vision totally consumed him. The chief of all apostles wanted to see the End as his Master predicted in Matthew 24:3 & 14. For example, when he was speaking to the Thessalonian Church about the rapture, he used the word "we" (referenced in the Scripture below), therefore, indicating that he envisaged he would be part of the generation that would be raptured.

> *"Then we which are alive and remain shall be caught up together with them in the clouds, to meet the Lord in the air: and so shall we ever be with the Lord." - 1 Thessalonians 4:17 (KJV)*

So what was Paul's strategy in pursuing the goal of finishing the Great Commission in his generation, and are there lessons for us today?

"yea, making it my aim so to preach the gospel, not where Christ was already named, that I might not build upon another man's foundation;" – Romans 15:20 (ASV)

"In all these, it has been my ambition to preach the Good News only where Christ's name was unknown." – Romans 15:20 (GSPD)

Paul's strategy was very clear: to preach the Gospel to those who have never heard it. His primary focus was to go to the regions beyond. So what do we mean when we speak of the regions beyond? They include:

- Where Christ has not been named
- The neglected fields
- The uttermost parts of the Earth
- Unoccupied areas
- Barren fields
- The other cities and the next towns

Again, Paul reiterates this same approach or strategy to doing ministry when he was writing to the Saints in Corinth.

"To preach the gospel in the regions beyond you, and not to boast in another man's line of things made ready to our hand." – 2 Corinthians 10:16 (KJV)

The question we should ask ourselves now is – how many Ministers and ministries share Paul's philosophy of ministry today? I know of a few ministries and Ministers whose primary focus is the unreached people groups. More often than not, these ministries and Ministers are not the popular names we all know as their work goes unnoticed. They are unsung heroes here on earth but Heaven's celebrities.

How else can we finish the Great Commission if not by taking the Gospel to the unreached people who do not have a Bible or Christian fellowship? Unfortunately, most Christian Ministers and Ministries don't have this philosophy of ministry or strategy. We are content with preaching to the same people, sometimes for decades.

Jesus' Strategy

I am almost certain that Paul's strategy of taking the Gospel to the regions beyond was inspired by the life of his Master, Jesus.

The Gospel of Mark, which is the Action Gospel, opens by presenting to the reader the exploits of Jesus. Unlike Matthew's Gospel that begins with the genealogy that traces Jesus' ancestral lineage just to prove that Jesus was the expected King of the Jews, Mark, as a lion, goes straight for the kill.

Jesus not only began His preaching and teaching ministry from the opening chapter, but His supernatural ministry was so impactful that His fame spread throughout all the regions round about Galilee. So popular did Jesus become that it is recorded that once the whole city was gathered at one of his meetings.

"And at even, when the sun did set, they brought unto him all that were diseased, and them that were possessed with devils. And all the city was gathered together at the door." – Mark 1:32-33 (KJV)

What occurs in the next few verses is worth paying attention to.

"And in the morning, rising up a great while before day, he went out, and departed into a solitary place, and there prayed. And Simon and they that were with him followed after him. And when they had found him, they said unto him, All men seek for thee. And he said unto them, Let us go into the next towns, that I may preach there also: for therefore came I forth." – Mark 1:35-38 (KJV)

What lessons can we learn from this passage? I believe a few:

First is the lesson on spiritual retreat. As Ministers, we must learn how to leave the stage and withdraw into solitude to be with the Father, particularly after major victories.

Second is the lesson on how to handle success and keep a focus on finishing the Great Commission. Did you notice what Simon said after he finally found Jesus –All men seek for thee (Mark 1:37). This was as a result of his successful outreach.

The question is "what would the 21st-century Evangelist or Pastor have done?" Many of us would have built a bigger building, increased the budget on publicity and media, and stayed there a lot longer.

I can imagine the excitement that would have overtaken Peter and all the disciples. What about Judas? He must have been calculating the financial breakthrough that would accrue to Jesus' Ministry as a result of the successful ministrations.

What Jesus did was so unconventional, and would have proved very unpopular - not just for the disciples, but the average 21st-century Preacher. Jesus must have said to them, "Guys, let's go to the next town. I'm talking about those who have never heard the Good News or felt the impact of my love."

> *"And he said unto them, Let us go into the next towns, that I may preach there also: for therefore came I forth." – Mark 1:38 (KJV)*

If we are going to finish the Great Commission in our generation, if we are going to be the generation that would witness the rapture and bring about the End, we must adopt as our strategy to always give our primary focus to the regions beyond – those who are in the next towns.

Practical Application for Finishing the Great Commission

1. If we are going to finish the Great Commission, churches and Believers must adopt, as their ministry goal, preaching in the regions beyond. Do you agree?

2. Can you identify a passage of Scripture where Jesus gave priority to those in the regions beyond?

3. What is your greatest obstacle against taking the Gospel to those in the regions beyond, and how can you overcome it?

CHAPTER 7

HOW WELL HAS THE CHURCH DONE?

Throughout my years as a student, the end of term was the most significant time, particularly after the examination period when results were about to be released. Often, students who put in their best efforts left school beaming with smiles whilst those who performed poorly had a sad demeanour. This experience goes to show the cause and effect relationship between efforts and rewards.

If the Church of Christ is at all concerned about finishing the Great Commission, it is important for us to reflect on how well we have done. In order to do this, I would like to make a few observations:

1. Firstly, when Jesus gave us the commission to go and disciple the nations, He wasn't speaking about geographical entities but ethnic groups. The best way to, therefore, assess how well we

are doing is to look at how many ethnic groups in the world have been reached with the Gospel. This is because Jesus declared that the End would not come until we have taken the Gospel to every ethnic group as a witness (Matthew 24:14).

2. Secondly, the majority of what we know today in world missions, particularly the unreached people groups, stems from extensive research that has been done by various organisations, and the advancement in technology and travel.

3. Thirdly, the figures that are given in this book are only estimates. This is because no one can be exact and figures are not static. They change as new information is available to research organisations.

4. Finally, these figures are meant to challenge and provoke us to act and get serious with the task of completing the Great Commission in our generation.

Statistics of the Unreached People Groups

According to the Joshua project,

- The world's population stands at 7.59 billion
- The total number of people groups is 17,017
- The unreached people groups are 7,087
- The total population among the unreached people groups is 3.14 billion, constituting about 41.4% of the world's population

It is worth noting that most of the unreached people groups are geographically located in what is referred to as "THE 10/40 WINDOW". This comprises the eastern hemisphere as well as the European and African parts of the western hemisphere that are located between 10 and 40 degrees north of the equator.

In reference to the figures above, we can deduce that for the past two thousand years, the Global Church has just been able to reach about 10,000 people groups with the Gospel. This leaves the remaining 3.14 billion unreached people in the dark, without Christ and no hope of eternal life. Is it, then, not alarming that the Church is unconcerned and fast asleep!

In order to appreciate fully how well the church is doing, let us look at the global statistics of Christianity.

Available statistics put the percentage of Christians as between 10 to 11% of the world's population! By this, we are referring to Bible-believing Christians. It is disheartening that if the rapture was to take place today, only 10% of the world's population would make Heaven and yet, Jesus died for the whole world! He tasted death for every human being and not a select few. In 1 Timothy 2:4 and 2 Peter 3:9, we read of how Christ desires that no man perishes.

> *"Who will have all men to be saved, and to come unto the knowledge of the truth." - 1 Timothy 2:4 (KJV)*

"The Lord is not slack concerning his promise, as some men count slackness; but is longsuffering to us-ward, not willing that any should perish, but that all should come to repentance." – 2 Peter 3:9 (KJV)

I once asked a congregation of Believers where I was preaching if they will celebrate if their child came home with their examination results, scoring 10%! Not surprisingly, the answer was a definite no. In the same vein, should the Church be celebrating for winning 10% of the world's population when Jesus died for all mankind? Some of you reading this book may protest that the Christian population should definitely be more than 10%. To make this much clearer, I will go on to explain in detail. The definition of Christians here refers to those who are genuinely born-again and are living according to the statutes of the Scriptures. Nominal Christians, on the other hand, are estimated at about 22% of the world's population, comprising those who profess the Christian Faith but are not necessarily living according to the statutes of the Word of God.

Since the thrust of this book is to challenge the Church to rise up to the challenge of world evangelisation, it would be appropriate to list some of the countries with the most unreached people groups. This, I believe should spur us on to restructure our global missions efforts.

Countries with the Most Unevangelised People

No.	Country	Unreached People Groups
1	India	2,222
2	Pakistan	448
3	China	427
4	Bangladesh	372
5	Nepal	355
6	Indonesia	200
7	Sudan	138
8	Laos	134
9	Iran	93
10	Russia	76
11	Thailand	76

- (Source Am TOP 10; www.aboutmissions.org)

Important Questions

There are a number of important questions that any Kingdom-loving, God-honouring Believer must reflect upon, in view of the above figures!

1. If indeed the total number of the unreached people groups stands at approximately 7,087 and India alone has over two thousand (2,222), Pakistan, 448, Bangladesh, 372 and Nepal, 355, where should the focus of the Global Church be?

2. In view of the above statistics, what percentage

of our budget should we be channelling to these countries?

3. The same applies to our ministry, travels and training. Where should we divert the focus of these to? Some ministries and para-church organisations have responded to the commission and are doing very well in reaching the unreached. However, the majority of Christians and Church leaders portray an indifferent attitude towards the plight of the unreached people.

I am always saddened when I read about the travel and ministry "exploits" of many Christian leaders, who focus all their attention and energies in the west - particularly Europe and North-America, yet would never give any attention to those who need the Gospel most.

To my brothers and sisters from Africa, I strongly believe it is our day in world missions. God is doing great things in the world today and in my estimation, the pendulum of world missions has shifted to the developing world, particularly Africa, Asia and South-America. Therefore, the Church in Africa must get more serious with the project of world missions and refrain from thinking that preaching in North-America and Europe is the ultimate in ministry. We must go to where the need is greatest.

We must take the injunction in Acts 1:8 seriously – "... *and ye shall be witnesses unto me both in Jerusalem, and in all Judaea, and in Samaria, and unto the uttermost part of the earth." (KJV).* As a result, we are to carry on reaching out at home and abroad concurrently.

It is also worth mentioning that apart from the primary focus being on the unreached people groups, the Church must next focus its attention, resources and prayers on those who might have heard the Gospel once but have never committed their lives to Christ. This includes nominal Christians, who constitute approximately 20% of the world's population. We must also strategise and target international students, who have come to study in the West, but their home countries are still closed to the Gospel, like North Korea and Saudi-Arabia. Once they are converted and discipled, they can be sent back home on assignment to further the cause of Christ.

The Church must target sinners wherever they may be found. Our priority must be to win all whom we possibly can and to also become all things to all men, like Paul, in order to win some. I have been to many church meetings, conferences and conventions where several thousands of pounds and dollars were spent, but the focus was not on sinners. We must change this attitude!

Perhaps it is best to conclude this chapter by reminding ourselves of the wise words of James Hudson Taylor, missionary to China, when he declared:

> *"The great commission is not an option to be considered; it is a command to be obeyed."*

Practical Application for Finishing the Great Commission

1. Why do you think Christians (including leaders) are not focusing on the unreached people groups, since we have enough information about them?

2. Do you believe that the pendulum of Christianity has shifted from the western world to the two-thirds world? If so, why is this?

3. Pentecostals and Charismatics bear a heightened responsibility for finishing the Great Commission. Do you agree with this statement?

4. Can you rate how well your local church is doing in world missions?

CHAPTER 8

WHY HAS THE CHURCH FAILED TO EVANGELISE THE WORLD?

After having received the commission to evangelise the world for over two thousand years, why have we failed to share the Good News around the world? There are many reasons that we can attribute to this failure. I would, however, want to highlight a few:

1. Gospel Recycling

"No one has the right to hear the Gospel twice, while there remains someone who has not heard it once"- Oswald J. Smith

Technological advancement has really helped modern life, particularly in the area of recycling. Today, unlike before, we are able to recycle our paper, plastic and cans etc. thus enabling us to make use of our resources more than once.

One of the greatest hindrances to finishing the Great Commission is Gospel recycling! Most Church leaders and ministries are simply recycling the Gospel by just focusing their ministry and message on the same people. One reason why I travel to the ends of the earth with the Gospel is that I don't think it is fair to feed the Gospel to the same people for several years without giving others a single opportunity to hear it.

"A tiny group of believers who have the gospel keep mumbling it over and over to themselves. Meanwhile, millions who have never heard it once fall into flames of eternal hell without ever hearing the story of salvation" K P. Yohannan

2. Pastoral Responsibilities

I have been involved directly in Pastoral ministry for about twenty-five years as this is something I love doing and forms part of my calling. Jesus commanded us to feed and take care of His flock. However, I am convinced that many Church leaders are too engrossed with pastoral duties such that they get into the maintenance mode and never have the time for missionary and evangelistic activities. I know of several Ministers of the Gospel who have never travelled out of their base, simply because the work-load of their ministry is just too much.

As Pastors, we must understand that we may be local, as far as our planting is concerned, but we must be global in our vision. The Gospel must, therefore, be preached both at home and abroad.

"But ye shall receive power, after that, the Holy Ghost is come upon you: and ye shall be witnesses unto me both in Jerusalem, and in all Judea, and in Samaria, and unto the uttermost part of the earth." - Act 1:8 (KJV)

3. Worldliness and Carnality

"Love not the world, neither the things that are in the world. If any man loves the world, the love of the Father is not in him. For all that is in the world, the lust of the flesh, and the lust of the eyes, and the pride of life, is not of the Father, but is of the world. And the world passeth away, and the lust thereof: but he that doeth the will of God abideth for ever." – 1 John 2:15-17 (KJV)

We cannot love the world and God at the same time! We will only love one and despise the other! Unfortunately, it is God that we often despise. When we speak of the world, we are referring to the systems of the world.

Did you know that money is the only competitor with God, and so often we bow to money rather than God? If you are in doubt, just reflect on how many hours we spend in a day pursuing money, and compare that with how many hours we spend with or for God. Do you know how much the modern-day gadgets have captured our hearts? I am speaking of mobile phones - with their attendant weapons of mass distraction ie. social media and television programs that Satan has released into the world. I have not seen or read of any other generation that is so self-centred like this generation.

Paul captured this vividly when he writes;

"This know also, that in the last days perilous times shall come. For men shall be lovers of their own selves, covetous, boasters, proud, blasphemers, disobedient to parents, unthankful, unholy," – 2 Timothy 3:1-2 (KJV)

"...lovers of pleasures more than lovers of God;"
- 2 Timothy 3:4b (KJV)

It's sad to note that today most Believers would rather indulge in worldly ventures than be busy with spiritual and eternal matters such as soul winning, praying, meditating and studying the Bible and other spiritual classics. Most Bible scholars and commentators agree that the Church is now in the Laodicean age – a Church that is lax, lukewarm, lazy, loose and lackadaisical! This Church is materially prosperous, but spiritually poor! (Revelation 2:14-22). What is the cumulative effect of all these? The Church becomes neutralized, and thus disinterested in spiritual things.

How many Believers do you know who have read some of the missions classics like *"From Jerusalem to Irian Jaya, God's Smuggler, A Force in the Earth, Transforming Missions and Eternity in Their Hearts"*, to mention these few.

4. A Shortage of Workers

One of the greatest problems militating against finishing the Great Commission is the shortage of workers on the field. According to the Joshua project, the status of Global Missions as at 2014, with regards to workers on the field, was as follows:

- There are approximately 7,000 unreached people groups
- 6.5 billion people are not followers of Jesus Christ
- The harvest force has 5,000,000 workers

in local churches, however, there are 700,000,000 followers of Jesus
- The Task in Perspective is to have:
  - 714 Local churches for every 1 unreached people group
  - 1 Follower of Jesus for every 10 Non-followers of Jesus

From these statistics, we can conclude that finishing the task is more achievable today than at any other time in history. The question we should be asking ourselves now is, why have we not been able to conclude it then? The simple answer being, labourers have not been released into the harvest field.

Many workers have simply refused to yield to the Master's call because of the comfort that they are enjoying in their home-church, while several others just prefer to go to over-saturated places! Jesus recognised this problem over two thousand years ago,

"... The harvest truly is plenteous, but the labourers are few; Pray ye therefore the Lord of the harvest, that he will send forth labourers into his harvest" – Matthew 9:37-38 (KJV)

To release the right labourers, many of them would need to undergo one form of missionary training or the other.

5. **Closed Doors**

While as churches we can be optimistic, it is also important to be realistic. Today, there are many nations of the world where it is a crime to share the Gospel or to even own a copy of the Bible! It is very dangerous to share the Gospel in places such as China, North Korea, and many of the Muslim states like Saudi-Arabia. Many Believers declare that there's no closed door to the Gospel because God cannot be legislated against. By His supernatural hand, we are seeing the manifestation of His wondrous works in these closed regions through unusual people. Where there have been restrictions, many Believers have gained entrance as tentmakers.

6. **The Lack of a Vision for Missions**

Everything starts with a vision! All the great missionary heroes and heroines were propelled to reach the heathen because they caught a vision. Mary Slessor, the missionary to Calabar in Nigeria once wrote, *"it was the dream of my girlhood to be a pioneer missionary."*

"Without vision, the people perish" - Hosea 4:6 (KJV)

The simple truth is that many church fellowships and genuine Servants of God are not involved in missions because they just don't have a vision for it. This is why we desperately need missions mobilisers to inspire and envision the sleeping giant. Sometimes, we need to encourage people to travel out of their comfort zone. It was as Jesus was travelling through all towns, cities and villages that He saw first-hand the condition of the people - sheep without a shepherd (Matthew 9:35).

7. Widespread Ignorance

Without a doubt, one of the reasons militating against the completion of World Harvest is the widespread ignorance of the Great Commission. According to the Barna Group, a Christian research organisation, 51% of Churchgoers in America don't know of the Great Commission (source - Barna group - March 2018). Despite the fact that Matthew 28, verses 18-20 is the most well known Biblical record of what is commonly referred to extra-biblically as "The Great Commission", over half of the Church population in America are unaware of these famous words from Jesus.

A few points need to be made first; this statistic only represents the Church in America, so it could be argued that this may not be a true representation of the Global Church. However, if we reflect on the fact that the Church in America is one of the most exposed, we might want to take this statistic seriously.

I very much doubt if the figures for Europe, which is post-Christian, would be close to that of America. The point is, if a high percentage of the Church is totally ignorant of the Great Commission, what hope do we have for completing it?

8. Because of Our Faulty Definition of Success

"For my thoughts are not your thoughts, neither are your ways my ways, saith the Lord. For as the Heavens are higher than the earth, so are my ways higher than your ways, and my thoughts than your thoughts." - Isaiah 55:8-9 (KJV)

A man's practices are always a by-product of his theology and philosophy. I believe the Church's progress in finishing the Great Commission has been greatly hampered because of what many Church leaders and Christians believe about success in ministry and Christian life.

Many years ago, to reckon that a Believer or Christian leader is successful, he or she must be living in obedience to God's Word and Will; they must be living the crucified life, they must give themselves to Christian discipline and virtues like prayer and fasting, giving and meditation, to mention a few. To be a successful Minister and ministry, you must take the Great Commission seriously, you must be regularly sending workers to the mission's field, praying for the expansion of God's kingdom, and giving towards the work of God.

Sadly enough, things have radically changed today. To be a successful Minister in this age, one must be seen hosting big conferences and inviting well-known speakers in Christendom. Success is also measured by one's popularity rating, particularly on social media, and the seating capacity of our churches but unfortunately not by the number of people we send out on missions or win into the body of Christ.

For the fortunes of Christ to change in the world today, a high percentage of Believers must change their philosophy of success from the materialistic viewpoint to that of obeying God's Word.

Practical Application for Finishing the Great Commission

1. What do we mean by "Gospel Recycling", and in your own words, how has this affected the completion of the Great Commission?

2. In what ways do you think Pastors can be freed from pastoral responsibilities in order to devote more time to the unsaved?

3. If you were to advise a group of Pastors and Church leaders in your city on how to complete the Great Commission in this generation, what would you be telling them?

CHAPTER 9

PREACHING THE GOSPEL OF THE KINGDOM

"You are either making disciples or making excuses. Which one are you?" - Jonathan Hayashi

"And this gospel of the kingdom shall be preached in all the world for a witness unto all nations; and then shall the end come." - Matthew 24:14 (KJV)

According to Jesus' own words, the end will only come after the Church has been faithful in preaching the Gospel of the Kingdom unto all nations! The question then is, why has the End not come after two thousand years of carrying out just one assignment? Could it be that the Church is not obeying Christ's own command to preach the Gospel of the Kingdom?

Are we really sure we understand what the Gospel of the Kingdom entails?

It is worth mentioning that there are 137 references to "the Kingdom" in the New Testament, and over 100 of these are during Jesus' Ministry. His entire teaching and approach as Messiah centres on this theme.

A close study of Jesus' Ministry reveals that He only preached the Gospel of the Kingdom (Matthew 3:2, 4:17).

John the Baptist, Jesus' fore-runner, also preached the same message. The Early Church centred their message on the Gospel of the Kingdom. For a proper understanding of the Gospel of the Kingdom, we need to appreciate its two dimensions.

1. The Gospel Of Salvation

"And she will bring forth a Son, and you shall call His name JESUS, for He will save His people from their sins." - Matthew 1:21 (NKJV)

The Gospel of Salvation encompasses wholeness, deliverance, healing, protection, provision and prosperity. Therefore when Jesus came, He brought us all these. One thing we must note is that The Gospel of Salvation is the entry point to the Kingdom.

From my personal observation, the focus of ministry in many parts of the world today has been the Gospel of Salvation. This is definitely true of most Pentecostal/charismatic ministries from Africa and the Caribbean.

What have the consequences been?

This Gospel makes us self-centred and reflects in our prayers and Christian activities which are inward-looking. In my estimation, this explains why so many Believers are immature, flaky, and need-driven. Most of our new generation ministries fall within this mould! Recently, there has been a growing criticism against many of these new ministries and Ministers because they seem not only to be too focused on material prosperity but also appear to be introverted, showing little or no concern for the plight of the poor.

If this Gospel is our primary focus and I believe it is for most ministries today in the world, particularly in Africa, then we are preaching a half-baked and incomplete Gospel!

2. The Social Gospel

The Social Gospel is the second dimension of the Gospel of the Kingdom. Just as every aeroplane has two wings for balance, so does the Gospel. For our Gospel to be authentic, that is the New Testament Gospel, it must have this second dimension! This is what I believe is missing in the 21st-century Church and is the fundamental reason why Jesus' coming has been delayed.

> "Then one of them, which was a lawyer, asked him a question, tempting him, and saying, Master, which is the great commandment in the

law? Jesus said unto him, Thou shalt love the Lord thy God with all thy heart, and with all thy soul, and with all thy mind. This is the first and great commandment. And the second is like unto it, Thou shalt love thy neighbour as thyself. On these two commandments hang all the law and the prophets." - Matthew 22:35-40 (KJV)

It is very instructive to note that Jesus connected and equalled the love for our neighbours to the Love of God with all our heart, strength and soul (emphasis - mine). Therefore it is impossible to love God and not love our neighbours. According to James 2:26, our Faith is dead without works ie. good works! Christians are meant to be "salt" and "light" in the world and not in the Church.

From the above, we can see that the Gospel of Salvation focuses on the individual's relationship with God and the meeting of their personal needs and sometimes greed. The Social Gospel, on the other hand, focuses on the needs of the community or our neighbours.

The Gospel of Salvation makes one 'inward-looking' while the Social Gospel makes one 'outward-looking'. This, in itself, is the thrust of real or true New Testament Christianity. This, to me, is one of the fundamental reasons why we have not completed the Great Commission and Jesus' coming has been greatly delayed.

Jesus did not just preach the message of salvation, but on numerous occasions, He met the physical or practical needs of the people - including feeding the multitudes!

The Early Church expanded and advanced the Gospel rapidly. Amongst the reasons for their success was the fact that it was a complete Gospel. Just like their Master, they not only preached the message of salvation, but they ministered to the needs of the poor, the least, last and the lost! They had, for example, a daily distribution which catered for the poor (Acts 6).

Historically, if we study the missionary activities of many mainland denominations like the Baptist, Anglican, Presbyterians, Methodists and Catholics, to mention these few, they brought a wholistic ministry - catering for the spiritual needs of their target groups via church fellowships, transforming the minds through the provisions of educational institutions and ministering to the physical needs through the building of hospitals, amongst many others.

To reach many unreached people today, we might have to first provide them with practical daily needs. Good News, to the hungry man, is feeding him! Those who are involved in front-line missionary activities know too well the impact that meeting practical needs has in unreached communities. I have seen first-hand myself, the way to people's hearts and homes are opened when you care for their practical needs.

Operation Mobilization, founded by George Verwer, has been able to reach many ethnic groups in the 10/40 window because of their ship ministry, which focuses on demonstrating Jesus' love by meeting practical needs.

The Gospel of the Kingdom is what I believe transformed Britain and made it Great. The pioneers of our Faith from this island didn't just proclaim the Good News, but they got involved in social justice, education, health, philanthropy etc. The same may be said for the United States of America. Unfortunately, Africa has a long way to go; even though many nations in the continent have been Christianised, the gains of the Gospel of the Kingdom have not been greatly reaped!

Landa Cope commented on this perplexing problem facing the African continent, in spite of the fact that Africa is the most evangelised continent. The poor people in most of the African states where Christianity has taken roots are becoming poorer. Her submission is that we are today reaping the harvest of preaching salvation alone at the expense of salvation and good works. She writes, *"The message that reformed western cultures and built nations on solidly Christian values was not the Gospel of salvation, but the Gospel of the kingdom, which includes salvation."*

"The truth of the Gospel of the kingdom is to transform us as they teach us how to live every part of our life. Our transformed lives are then to be salt and light to our families, neighbours, communities and finally our nations, making them better places to live for everyone. Not perfect communities, not Heaven on earth, but better

because the influence of good is as great, if not greater than evil" - Missional Reformation, A. Olowe, p136, Omega Publishers, Houston U.S.A: 2009.

Practical Application for Finishing the Great Commission

1. What does the Gospel of the Kingdom entail?
2. The Social Gospel will be the key to opening up many unreached peoples. Do you agree?
3. Can you identify some lessons that the 21st-century Church can learn from the missionaries that took the Gospel to Africa, Asia and the Caribbean?

CHAPTER 10

WHY WIN SOULS?

If the Church is to finish the Great Commission in our generation, it is imperative that every Believer and indeed every church fellowship understands the reason why we must be passionate soul winners. Most of us tend to perform better when we appreciate or understand the reasons for our actions. The following represents some of the reasons why I believe every Believer ought to be a soul winner:

1. It Is A Command

The Great Commission is not a piece of advice, but a command. Soul winning, therefore, cannot be reduced to being just a nice thing to do; it's an order! Believers don't have an option - you are either obeying or disobeying Christ's command.

"The Christian is not obedient unless he is doing all in his power to send the Gospel to the heathen world." – A.B. Simpson

2. To Demonstrate Our Love For God

If we genuinely love God, we would definitely obey His commands. One of the clearest and dearest commands of Christ to His Church is to share the Gospel to all mankind.

"If ye love me, keep my commandments." – John 14:15 (KJV)

"He that hath my commandments, and keepeth them, he it is that loveth me: and he that loveth me shall be loved of my Father, and I wil love him, and will manifest myself to him." – John 14:21 (KJV)

Can we genuinely claim to love a person without making every effort to do those things that are pleasing to them? Our love for God is not just manifested when we sing, dance, or even give. We can measure our love for God on how well we are obeying His command.

3. We Are Debtors

Preaching the Gospel and thereby winning souls into the Kingdom of God is a debt we owe as Christians.

"We are debtors to every man; to give him the gospel in the same measure in which we have received it." – Phineas F. Bresee

When you borrow something, like money from the bank, you become a debtor, and are under obligation to repay it. I presently have a mortgage on my home and as a result, I am obliged not just to meet my monthly repayment, but to fully settle the debt to the very last pound!

Until the Church sees the Great Commission as a debt that we owe to about 30% of the world's population who have never heard the name of Jesus Christ, and the billions of people who have never made a decision for Him, we would never take this commission seriously!

I am convinced that it was this unique revelation that made Paul, the Apostle, Primus inter pares when it comes to obeying Christ's last command.

"I am debtor both to the Greeks, and to the Barbarians; both to the wise, and to the unwise."
– Romans 1:14 (KJV)

4. Because Of The Value Of Souls

If there's something that the Church of the 21st-century must appreciate more, it is the value of souls. May God open the eyes of our understanding so that we may appreciate this. If I were to ask you - what is your most valuable asset? I would probably get different answers ranging from business, job, family, houses, education, money, and the list would be endless. Let's explore this issue a bit further. What makes a thing valuable?

The Creator - the person who makes or creates a product, thing or service determines its value.

Longevity – the value of a product or commodity would be affected by its lifespan.

Substitutability– again, we must ask the all-important question - does the product have substitutes and if so, how easily accessible are they? If not, the product or service will be more valuable.

Did you know that a person's soul is the most valuable asset he/she possesses? Its creator is God Himself and there is no substitute for it as our souls are eternal. In 100 billion years from today, my soul, for example, will still be in existence while all the material things I might have acquired in my lifetime – money, cars, degrees, houses etc., would have perished or gone into extinction. No wonder Jesus raised this salient question:

> *"For what shall it profit a man, if he shall gain the whole world, and lose his own soul? Or what shall a man give in exchange for his soul?"*
> *– Mark 8:36-37 (KJV)*

I once reflected on the glories of this world - beautiful homes, islands, cars, trains, aeroplanes, gold, diamond, etc. and concluded that none of these can match up to the value of a man's soul. In fact, if we put everything in this world together - its treasures and glory, its combined value is still pale in comparison to the soul of man. This was why Jesus raised the question above. Not surprisingly, the answer is definitely nothing! Can we now appreciate how precious it is to have the privilege of leading an erring soul back to its maker? In conclusion, a soul is priceless!

5. Because We Need To Please God

Among the many things that motivated Paul in being a soul winner per excellence was his all-consuming desire to please God. Today, many Christians do everything to please and get the approval of people; their spouse, friends, colleagues, employers, and often their spiritual guides or mentors. As good as all these may be, a day is coming when what would really count is whether or not we have lived a life pleasing to our creator.

> *"Wherefore we labour, that, whether present or absent, we may be accepted of him." – 2 Corinthians 5:9 (KJV)*

There's no way a Christian who never won a soul, or took evangelism and missions seriously would be accepted by God.

6. Jesus Is The Only Way To God

As Believers, we must be addicted soul winners because there's only one way to God which is through

Christ Jesus. Every other way will lead to death and damnation.

> *"Jesus saith unto him, I am the way, the truth, and the life: no man cometh unto the Father, but by me."*- John 14:6 (KJV)

7. The Glory Of God

Perhaps the most overlooked or underplayed motive for winning souls into the Kingdom of God is the Glory of God. Do you realise that anytime a soul is won, God is being honoured and glorified? Reconciling Adam's fallen race back to its maker is all about the Glory of God.

Count Nikolaus Ludwig Von Zinzendorf, the leader of the Moravians, discovered and emphasised this motive by challenging his followers to *"win for the Lamb the reward of His sacrifice!"*

The Westminster short catechism asks the question: *"what is the chief purpose of man?"*. Its response is, *"to live for His glory and to enjoy Him forever!"*

The greatest offering of worship we can give to King Jesus is to bring souls to Him.

8. The Lostness Of Man

> *Jesus declared "For the Son of man is come to seek and to save that which was lost." – Luke 19:10 (KJV)*

Many people in our world today believe that by just being sincere, they will get to Heaven; nothing can be farther from the truth. The picture that the Scriptures paint of a man outside of Christ is grim. They're not only lost but also without hope. Today, there is a widespread belief in universalism which teaches that "all would ultimately be saved". This is not only false but unscriptural. If everyone would ultimately be saved, then surely there would be no need for us to preach the Gospel. It doesn't matter our education, dogma or achievements, outside of Jesus, we are eternally lost and damned.

9. Spiritual Growth

Nothing aids or promotes one's spiritual growth more than being an active soul winner. I am yet to come across a soul winner who is not a growing Christian. I say this because as a diligent soul winner, you will find yourself always praying, meditating, studying the Word of God and attending fellowship regularly with other Saints. Personally, sharing my Faith from the moment I gave my life to Christ has been one of the keys to my spiritual growth. As I shared my Faith and testimony, I had to go and study, meditate on Scriptures, fast and pray. These disciplines, I believe, have helped me grow over the years.

10. Hell is Real

This is the verdict of the holy writ. Hell is a place that exists, and the picture that the Bible paints of it is not pleasant at all. Even Jesus spoke more about Hell than Heaven while here on earth. All the major religions believe in Hell, however, Christianity is the only religion that provides a solution through Christ. Some have argued that Hell is simply a figment of man's imagination, while others have claimed that it is only a metaphoric expression. The Bible is unequivocal, not only about the reality of Hell but the candidates - the wicked; those who never washed themselves in the blood; all those whose names are not written in the Book of life.

> *"The wicked shall be turned into hell, and all the nations that forget God." – Psalm 9:17 (KJV)*

> *"And whosoever was not found written in the book of life was cast into the lake of fire." – Revelation 20:15 (KJV)*

> *"But the fearful, and unbelieving, and the abominable, and murderers, and whoremongers, and sorcerers, and idolaters, and all liars, shall have their part in the lake which burneth with fire and brimstone: which is the second death." – Revelation 21:8 (KJV)*

Jesus presented the clearest picture of Hell when he spoke in Luke 16:19- 31, about the story of Lazarus and the rich man.

A few facts about Hell:

1. Our senses will still be very active in Hell.
2. It is definitely a place of torment and regrets.
3. There is a gulf fixed such that once you are in Hell, you can't change your location or status.
4. The way you live your life on earth is what will determine whether you will end up in Hell or not.

It is worth reiterating that many roads lead to Hell, but there are no exits. Apart from the gloomy picture that the Bible paints, I have heard several testimonies of people who have been privileged to visit Hell – every single person has dramatically altered their lives as a result of the gory experience they went through. One of my greatest motivations for preaching the Gospel and challenging Believers across the world to do same is the severity of the torment in Hell.

I am totally convinced that the majority of Christians, and indeed Pastors, don't believe in the reality of Hell. If we claim otherwise, then our actions, lukewarmness and indifference towards the plight of the lost, is most pitiable.

11. Fruitfulness
God demands that His children are fruitful.

> *"Herein is my Father glorified, that ye bear much fruit; so shall ye be my disciples." – John 15:8 (KJV)*

True disciples bear fruits and so in essence, genuine followers of Christ are soul winners. I often hear Believers testify of how powerful and impactful the conventions and meetings they attend are; yet at these gatherings, no souls are won, or disciples made and no challenge is given for the Good News to be taken to the next towns, cities and nations. You would agree with me when I say that no farmer will be satisfied with planting seeds without harvesting the yield! Likewise, no fisherman will come home excited without a catch! God is not pleased and there is no celebration in Heaven when we fail to win souls.

12. God's Emergency Service

Another important reason why Christians must be soul winners is that we constitute God's emergency service. From the day we became born-again, we were conscripted into God's rescue force. Just as the police, ambulance and fire services are trained to be rescue operators that save people from danger, so also are we called to save souls from eternal damnation. The interesting fact about emergency workers is that they are trained to appreciate the urgency of the hour. Many have risked their lives countless times in an attempt to save others. It's disheartening to recognise that many Christians do not respond with this kind of speed, compassion and diligence when it comes to the plight of perishing souls. The truth is, most Christians do not even perceive themselves as God's rescue operators.

I have lived in the United Kingdom for over 26 years, and I have watched firsthand how our emergency services respond to life-threatening situations. They really put me to shame when I compare their sense of urgency to mine.

It was Fanny J. Crosby, 1869, who wrote the famous hymn:

> *Rescue the perishing, care for the dying,*
> *Snatch them in pity from sin and the grave;*
> *Weep o'er the erring one, lift up the fallen,*
> *Tell them of Jesus, the mighty to save.*

> *Refrain:*
> *Rescue the perishing, care for the dying,*
> *Jesus is merciful, Jesus will save.*

> *Though they are slighting Him, still He is waiting,*
> *Waiting the penitent child to receive;*
> *Plead with them earnestly, plead with them gently;*
> *He would forgive if they only believe.*
> *[Refrain]*

> *Down in the human heart, crushed by the tempter,*
> *Feelings lie buried that grace can restore;*
> *Touched by a loving heart, wakened by kindness,*
> *Chords that were broken will vibrate once more.*
> *[Refrain]*

Rescue the perishing, duty demands it;
Strength for thy labor the Lord will provide;
Back to the narrow way patiently win them;
Tell the poor wand'rer a Savior has died.
[Refrain]

13. False Religions And Cults Are Doing The Job

One thing that puts me to shame or challenges me more is when I come across people of other faiths or what many true Believers will consider as cults, doing exactly what Jesus has commanded us to do. I am almost convinced that no matter where you are living, you most likely would have come into contact with the Jehovah's Witnesses (JW) or the Church of Jesus Christ of Latter-day Saints (Mormons). It doesn't matter the time of year or how harsh the weather conditions are, the JW's are always on the go. They are knocking at doors with their tracts and literature; at train stations, shopping malls, etc. I am told that the Mormons are encouraged to give two years of their lives to missions. I pray that day will come fast when the average member of our congregations will volunteer to take the Gospel to foreign fields for two years; then, we can be assured that it won't be long before Jesus comes.

Islam is growing at an alarming rate in Britain and throughout the western world which used to be a Christian preserve. Our churches are being bought and turned into mosques, simply because they are serious with the devil's commission to populate Hell! Little wonder that Jesus declared that *"... the children of this world are in their generation wiser than the children of light." – Luke 16:8 (KJV)*

14. It's Harvest Time and the Time is Short!

"Say not ye, There are yet four months, and then cometh harvest? behold, I say unto you, Lift up your eyes, and look on the fields; for they are white already to harvest." – John 4:35 (KJV)

Did you notice what Jesus said about the harvest fields from the above passage? They are already white, meaning it's time to harvest; it's time to go to the nations; it's time to go to the highways and byways to compel men and women to come in. If the fields were ripe 2000 years ago according to Jesus, how much truer is this assertion today? All signs around us today point to the fact that God is wrapping up everything; prophecies are being fulfilled before our very eyes.

As I write, Ezekiel 38 and 39 are being fulfilled – Russia, Turkey, Iran, Syria, and other nations are forming alliances, getting ready to attack Israel. Israel has become a cup of trembling to the whole world, including the United Nations. Knowledge is increasing at such a rate that we cannot even keep up, thanks to technological advancement and media breakthrough. The President of the United States has just declared Jerusalem as the eternal capital of Israel. Iniquity and lawlessness is now the order of the day. There is spiritual apathy and lukewarmness in the Church like I have never seen in over three decades of preaching the Gospel. North Korea, which has been totally closed to the Gospel, might be opening its gateways anytime from now - thanks to the breakthrough coming up between the American and North Korean leaders. Unfortunately, most Believers cannot read the signs on the wall.

We must become the sons of Issachar, who were men that had an understanding of the times, and knew what Israel ought to do (1 Chronicles 12:32a).

Peter declared that the end of all things is at hand. *"But the end of all things is at hand: be ye therefore sober, and watch unto prayer." – 1 Peter 4:7 (KJV)*

In view of the times we live in, what in your opinion should be our primary focus and assignment? As far as I am concerned it must be souls, souls and more SOULS!!! Every convention, board meeting, or church anniversary celebration should be an occasion for us to focus our attention on the all-important assignment of completing the Great Commission in our generation.

15. Only One Life!
"I have but one candle of life to burn, and I would rather burn it out in a land filled with darkness than in a land flooded with light" –
John Keith Falconer

One of the greatest reasons why every Christian must take the Great Commission mandate seriously is because we only have one shot at life. We all only have one life to prove to God how much we love him. What a privilege we have when most people are trying to invest their lives in temporal mundane and fleeting things. There's no better way to live our lives than to invest it in the most rewarding venture of soul winning! I look back often and I regret not putting in more time, greater effort and multiple resources.

In the same vein, once a sinner is dead, the door to Heaven is eternally shut. There is no second chance. As you're reading this book, can you think of the number of people who have died today, this week, month and year, in your neighbourhood, town, city, nation, and the entire globe, who have gone to a Christ-less and hopeless eternity? Friend, we have only one life! By all means, we must make sure it counts by investing our time in fulfilling the Great Commission.

"And as it is appointed unto men once to die, but after this the judgment:" - Hebrews 9:27 (KJV)

16. Divine Accountability And Sanctions
"Someone asked, will the heathen who have never heard the Gospel be saved? It is more a question with me whether we - who have the Gospel and fail to give it to those who have not - can be saved"- Charles Spurgeon

Supposing there was a fire outbreak in your neighbour's house and you were privileged to witness it starting out, however, you walked past without alerting your neighbour. Eventually, the whole house got burnt and a family of five died in the inferno. Would you have been thanked by your neighbour and the society? Definitely not! You would be judged as being extremely wicked and possibly serve jail time. Again, if you have the cure to cancer, would you keep it to yourself and leave millions to die needlessly? I doubt that.

One thing I hardly hear on our pulpits today is the reality of God holding to account all who refuse to share the Gospel. Yes! You read this right - there will be divine sanctions for all who had the opportunity to share the Gospel with the dying world but kept it to themselves. Let's consider one of such Scriptures:

> *"If thou forbear to deliver them that are drawn unto death, and those that are ready to be slain; if thou sayest, Behold, we knew it not; doth not he that pondereth the heart consider it? and he that keepeth thy soul, doth not he know it? and shall not he render to every man according to his works?" - Proverbs 24:11-12 (KJV)*

God is watching our response to those who are being drawn to death all around us. For sure as the Scriptures declare, He is going to reward all of us one day according to our works.

Again, I am convinced that many Believers will get to Heaven, and rather than being overjoyed, they will have moments of regret and tears will fill their eyes as they open up their hands to see the blood of those they should have shared the Gospel with but never did. God's commission and challenge to Prophet Ezekiel should always serve as a warning to every serious Believer:

> *"Son of man, I have made thee a watchman unto the house of Israel: therefore hear the word at my mouth, and give them warning from me. When I say unto the wicked, Thou shalt surely die; and thou givest him not warning, nor speakest to warn the wicked from his wicked way, to save his life; the same wicked man shall die in his iniquity; but his blood would I require at thine hand. Yet if thou warn the wicked, and he turn not from his wickedness, nor from his wicked way, he shall die in his iniquity; but thou hast delivered thy soul." - Ezekiel 3:17-19 (KJV)*

It is very clear that God will not hold us guiltless if we know the truth about the danger ahead of sinners and yet refuse to warn them.

> *"Again the word of the LORD came unto me, saying, Son of man, speak to the children of thy people, and say unto them, When I bring the sword upon a land, if the people of the land*

take a man of their coasts, and set him for their watchman: If when he seeth the sword come upon the land, he blow the trumpet, and warn the people; Then whosoever heareth the sound of the trumpet, and taketh not warning; if the sword come, and take him away, his blood shall be upon his own head. He heard the sound of the trumpet, and took not warning; his blood shall be upon him. But he that taketh warning shall deliver his soul. But if the watchman see the sword come, and blow not the trumpet, and the people be not warned; if the sword come, and take any person from among them, he is taken away in his iniquity; but his blood would I require at the watchman's hand. So thou, O son of man, I have set thee a watchman unto the house of Israel; therefore thou shalt hear the word at my mouth, and warn them from me." - Ezekiel 33:1-7 (KJV)

It is very clear, from the above passage that God will hold us accountable for those we have the opportunity of sharing the Gospel with and have refused to. What about your immediate neighbours, colleagues, business and workmates, family members, and those living at the uttermost parts of the world? Have you made attempts to share the Gospel or are you simply looking away? Is God not watching us, and would He not reward us according to our deeds? May God help us!

17. Because Soul winners are Joyful People

"To be a soul winner is the happiest thing in the world. And with every soul you bring to Jesus Christ, you seem to get a new Heaven here upon earth" - Charles Spurgeon

Soul winners are often happy and joyful people! By no means are they immune from challenges, temptations and satanic onslaughts. However, when you meet a soul winner, they radiate with contagious joy that can't be compared to anything. Anytime I win a soul, I am fulfilled and filled with unspeakable joy.

The Bible records the joy that accompanies the fulfilment of the Great Commission when Jesus sent out His seventy disciples:

"And the seventy returned again with joy, saying, Lord, even the devils are subject unto us through thy name." - Luke 10:17 (KJV)

18. The Majority of Christians Will Never Take Soul winning and Finishing The Great Commission Seriously

"You may not be allowed to stand on the pulpit in your church to preach, but every junction in your area is a pulpit. Stand there and preach" – Reinhard Bonnke

This is a fact! Most Believers are not soul winners. Even most Christian leaders are not passionate about completing the Great Commission in their generation. Many Church leaders have been startled anytime I share the statistics of the unreached people and those outside the fold. We Christians find it very easy here in the West to go on holiday but will hardly ever consider going abroad on missions. Scriptures declare that "… many are called, but few are chosen." – Matthew 22:14 (KJV). As the majority of God's children will not answer His call for world missions, the responsibility now rests upon the few who will respond to double their efforts.

19. Eternal Rewards

The God of the Bible is a master motivator. He always motivates us to do the right things and then promises rewards. Have you noticed that people tend to do better and even stretch themselves to the limits when they are motivated with a reward? Corporations, businesses and educational institutions always promise rewards in order to motivate their members to achieve greater productivity and excellence. In the same vein, God motivates us to spread the Gospel as far as we can in order to win precious souls.

So, how does God motivate us? There are eternal rewards – glories and crowns reserved for only soul winners:

"And they that be wise shall shine as the brightness of the firmament; and they that turn

many to righteousness as the stars for ever and ever." - Daniel 12:3 (KJV)

Who are they that would shine as the brightness of the firmament? Indeed soul winners are the ones that will turn many to righteousness and receive the reward of shinning like stars forever.

In my study of the Scriptures, I have discovered that there are at least five crowns that the Lord will be awarding to Believers at the BEMA seat for the way they lived while on earth. There is a crown specifically reserved for soul winners which is called "the Crown of Rejoicing"

"For what is our hope, or joy, or crown of rejoicing? Are not even ye in the presence of our Lord Jesus Christ at his coming?" - 1 Thessalonians 2:19 (KJV)

One of my greatest motivations for taking the Gospel to the nations is to receive the Crown of Rejoicing.

Some years ago, I made a commitment in prayer to God to try to win at least one soul from every nation on this earth by me going, giving or praying. How amazing would it be for one to get to Heaven and meet nationals from every nation coming to thank you for the part you played in making them get to Heaven?

Let me end this chapter by sharing with you a challenge from one of God's greatest missionary statesmen of the 20th century - Dr Oswald J Smith (1889 - 1986)

"Give us a watchword for the hour,
A thrilling word, a word of power;
A battle cry, a flaming breath,
That calls to conquest or to death;
A word to rouse the church from rest,
To heed the Master's strong request
The call is given, ye hosts arise,
Our watchword is Evangelise!
The glad Evangel now proclaim
Through all the Earth, in Jesus' name;
This word is ringing through the skies;
Evangelise! Evangelise!!
To dying men, a fallen race,
Make known the gift of Gospel grace.
To the world that now in darkness lies,
Evangelise! Evangelise!!"

Practical Application for Finishing the Great Commission

1. Can you state 4 important reasons why Christians need to win souls?
2. What reason(s) challenges you the most for winning souls, and why?
3. What changes do you have to make to become a better soul winner?

CHAPTER 11

PRAYER AND WORLD-EVANGELISATION

What is the correlation between prayer and world evangelisation? Do prayers and intercession play any significant role in finishing the Great Commission?

Anyone who is serious about finishing the Great Commission would accede to the fact that prayer is the most strategic, but yet unused force. If there's one thing that church history has proved, it is that progress in missionary endeavours has been fuelled by consistent, aggressive, heartfelt prayers by the Church. The Early Church not only grew exponentially through daily conversions, but they took new territories for God. The secret, Prayer!

"These all continued with one accord in prayer and supplication, with the women, and Mary

*the mother of Jesus, and with his brethren." -
Acts 1:14 (KJV)*

*"And they continued steadfastly in the apostles'
doctrine and fellowship, and in breaking of
bread, and in prayers." - Acts 2:42 (KJV)*

*"But we will give ourselves continually to
prayer, and to the ministry of the word." - Acts
6:4 (KJV)*

The Moravians

*"I have but one passion - It is He, it is He alone.
The world is the field, and the field is the world;
and henceforth that country shall be my home
where I can be most used in winning souls for
Christ" - Count Nikolaus Ludwig Von Zinzendorf*

Count Nikolaus Ludwig Von Zinzendorf led one of
the greatest missionary movements of all time - the
Moravians. He was born into a family that was one of
the most ancient of noble families in Austria. At the age
of 6, he fell in love with Jesus and continued to mature in
the Lord. In May 1721, he purchased his grandmother's
estate at Berthelsdorf, where everything changed for
him when Moravian refugees began to arrive at the
manor. It started off with Christian David and by May
1725, 90 Moravians had settled at Herrnhut, growing to
about 300 by late 1726.

100-Year Prayer Watch

The year 1727 marked a turning point in the Moravian community. On August 5th, the Count spent the whole night in prayer with about 12-14 others. A few days later on August 13th, the Holy Spirit was poured out on them just like the Day of Pentecost. This experience radically changed the whole community and sparked a flame of prayer and missions that would last for over 100 years. This was the beginning of the non-stop 24-hour prayer movement regarded to be the longest prayer movement in history! What was their prayer focus? Very simple - Revival and missionary expansion.

What was the effect of this prayer movement? History records that from the time of the commencement of the prayers, the Moravians sent missionaries out unto all the world - some of them even sold themselves as slaves in order to take the Gospel to foreign lands. One thing many may be unaware of was the influence of the Moravians on John Wesley. It was Wesley's encounter with a group of Moravians on his way to Georgia that led to his search for an inward reality.

A House of Prayer for All Nations

"And said unto them, It is written, My house shall be called the house of prayer; but ye have made it a den of thieves." - Matthew 21:13 (KJV)

One day, Jesus went into the temple on a cleansing campaign! He overthrew the tables of money changers and the seats of those selling doves, rebuking them for misusing the House of God! If Jesus were to be here today, I believe He would be doing same - cleansing His house! Anyone with any spiritual discernment will agree that the Church today desperately needs spiritual cleansing. We have turned the House of God into business empires and political platforms. We seem to be more concerned with money and material things than souls and kingdom advancement. After the cleansing, Jesus declared the true purpose of His house (the Church); a house of prayer! Yes, a house of prayer.

Our primary assignment is to be a house of prayer! The one million dollar question is - are we praying right? Without a doubt, many ministries, churches and Ministers seem to be praying! Throughout the year, we have prayer emphasis days, weeks and months. There are ministries that I know personally that have prayer and fasting every year for about 100 days. Often, our prayer focus and topics seem to be geared towards PERSONAL NEEDS!

Prophet Isaiah declares a central component of God's House which is prayer for the nations.

> *"These I will bring to my holy mountain and give them joy in my house of prayer. Their burnt offerings and sacrifices will be accepted on my altar; for my house will be called a house of prayer for all nations." - Isaiah 56:7 (NIV)*

Did you notice how God describes His house? It's a house of prayer for all nations! Today, we have turned God's House to a house of prayer for individual needs. The 21st-century Church has become so self-centred and need-driven that we look so pathetic when compared to the Early Church.

It seems the only way to fill our auditoriums and get people interested in the things of God is to focus the attention on individuals and their insatiable wants. Never will I be against praying for individual needs, however, when it distracts and consumes us above our primary assignment, it must be put to question.

What did Jesus mean by His house shall be called a house of prayer for all nations? It means we must constantly be praying for all the nations and people groups for their salvation; that the glorious Gospel would penetrate into their hearts and communities. Can we imagine what would happen in our world today if all ministries and church fellowships consistently pray for all the unreached people groups?

Jesus' Recommendation to Unlocking The End-time Harvest

Jesus gave the Church the Master Key to completing the assignment He entrusted to us over two thousand years ago; which is prayer.

> "And Jesus went about all the cities and villages, teaching in their synagogues, and preaching

the gospel of the kingdom, and healing every
sickness and every disease among the people.
But when he saw the multitudes, he was moved
with compassion on them, because they fainted,
and were scattered abroad, as sheep having no
shepherd. Then saith he unto his disciples, The
harvest truly is plenteous, but the labourers are
few; Pray ye therefore the Lord of the harvest,
that he will send forth labourers into his
harvest." - Matthew 9:35-38 (KJV)

From the above passage, we can see clearly Jesus'
recommendation to solve the harvest challenge.
Surely, it wasn't by fundraising, strategizing or having
committee meetings. A hundred times NO! While all
these may be excellent, Jesus' recommendation was
prayer - "Pray ye!" We are, therefore, to petition the
Lord of the Harvest and in response to our prayers, He
will thrust or push labourers out.

There are many labourers who will only respond to
the call if they are forced out by God. This occurred in
Acts 8, verses 1 to 4, when God allowed persecution to
disperse the Early Church, and in so doing took the Good
News out of the boundaries of the city of Jerusalem.

Countries and Not Cars!

"Ask of me, and I shall give thee the heathen
for thine inheritance, and the uttermost parts of
the earth for thy possession." - Psalms 2:8 (KJV)

110

Our sin-loving, self-serving and God-dishonouring generation would rather petition Heaven for carnal and transient things than request treasures that would last for eternity. The above promise is from God the Father to His son, and by extension to all who will pray right. Rather than claim cars, we should be claiming countries or nations as our inheritance! Regularly, I petition Heaven for God to give me souls and fruits from every nation on earth.

It truly disturbs me when I see Believers and even Church leaders testify and brag about their latest "machine" - all as a sign of God's blessing or approval. Why can't we brag about nations and souls?

God must raise up again kingdom-minded Saints who would desire nothing other than nations, cities, towns and villages - Men like John Knox who prayed continuously - *"God, give me Scotland or I die"*.

John Praying Hyde of India was an Apostle of prayer. He was the man that prayed the famous prayer – *"O God, give me souls, lest I die."* This was his constant prayer. He loved spending time with his Lord and Saviour in prayer, often missing meals and sleep. He prayed each day, give me a soul or I die! God indeed answered his prayer as daily a soul was saved. Later he asked God for two, then for four and lastly, eight. Here was a man greatly used by God for revivals which ushered several thousands of souls in India into the Body of Christ.

He died at the young age of 47. When an autopsy was done on him, they found out that his heart had moved from the left to the right side - all out of an agony and burden for souls.

Are You an Unbelieving Believer?

"Therefore I say unto you, Take no thought for your life, what ye shall eat, or what ye shall drink; nor yet for your body, what ye shall put on. Is not the life more than meat, and the body than raiment?

Behold the fowls of the air: for they sow not, neither do they reap, nor gather into barns; yet your heavenly Father feedeth them. Are ye not much better than they?

Which of you by taking thought can add one cubit unto his stature? And why take ye thought for raiment? Consider the lilies of the field, how they grow; they toil not, neither do they spin: And yet I say unto you, That even Solomon in all his glory was not arrayed like one of these.

Wherefore, if God so clothe the grass of the field, which to day is, and to morrow is cast into the oven, shall he not much more clothe you, O ye of little faith?

Therefore take no thought, saying, What shall we eat? or, What shall we drink? or, Wherewithal shall we be clothed? (For after all these things do the Gentiles seek:) for your heavenly Father knoweth that ye have need of all these things.

> *But seek ye first the kingdom of God, and*
> *his righteousness; and all these things shall be*
> *added unto you. - Matthew 6:25-33 (KJV)*

Jesus warned Believers not to focus or preoccupy themselves with their needs – eating, drinking, clothing, etc. In fact, we are to take no thought of these things, talk less of making them a prayer point. The simple reason is that our Heavenly Father is aware we have need of them! If He can take care of nature, how much more his children?

We are to seek first God's kingdom and its righteousness, and everything will follow suit. Isn't it amazing that most of our prayer requests, seminars and conventions are centred around our needs and yet we have been commanded to pay no thought to them! Why then are we behaving like the Gentiles or unbelievers whose primary preoccupation is to meet their daily needs!

The more we seek the Kingdom by praying for its expansion, the more our personal needs will be met. Essentially, when we make God's business our priority, we can be confident that He will make our business His business.

Would you respond to the challenge of praying for the end-time Harvest?

Practical Application for Finishing the Great Commission

1. Prayer is the most unused force or resource in world evangelisation! Comment.
2. Most Christians and church fellowships are self-centred in their prayers. Do you agree?
3. What is the role of Pastors and Church leaders in channelling prayers into world evangelisation?

CHAPTER 12

FUNDING THE GREAT COMMISSION

"Today, Christians spend more money on dog food than missions." – Leonard Ravenhill

"Jesus will judge us not only for what we did, but also for what we could have done but didn't do." – George Otis

"Love is the root of missions; sacrifice is the fruit of missions." – Roderick Davis

It is impossible writing on an important subject like completing the Great Commission without reflecting on how to fund such a worthy and lofty enterprise. To take the Good News to the ends of the earth would not only cost billions of dollars but also require a change in the giving pattern of most Believers. I must confess that I am the least qualified to write about this topic because, in my own estimation, I believe I can give much more than I already do to further the work of the Kingdom.

In this chapter, I would like to argue not just for more giving by the average Christian, but a much higher percentage must be directed towards missions, particularly the unreached people groups.

This theme of generosity towards missions received prominence in one of the concluding chapters of "The Cape Town Commitments" (Lausanne Movement) that emerged from Cape Town in 2010. It states:

> *"Biblical mission demands that those who claim Christ's name should be like Him by taking up their cross, denying themselves, and following Him in the paths of humility, love, integrity, generosity and servanthood."*

Many Church leaders today believe that there is enough money and resources in the Church to complete the Great Commission. The problem, according to them is the lack of proper administration. In an article on how Christians spend their money (source – IMBR 2013), Russ Mitchell presents the fact about Christian giving and expenditure globally.

The report highlights that the personal income of Christians globally is estimated to be over 33 trillion dollars. 594 billion dollars (a paltry 1.8% of personal income) was given to all Christian causes. Ecclesiastical Crime (embezzlement and misappropriation of funds for personal gain) cost 37 billion dollars, while 33 billion dollars was allocated for world missions. More money is embezzled from Christian causes than is spent on world missions. A bit more than a half of a penny out of every dollar of Christian giving goes to world missions (0.575 cents to be exact).

In a report by "The Bibles for All the World Prayer Map", 95% of American Christian giving remains in the country for home-based ministry, 4.5% goes to outreach programmes in already evangelised nations and 0.5% only goes to the unreached people groups.

In a similar vein, the U.S. centre for world missions reports that only 5.7% of giving to Christian causes goes to foreign missions. Of that, 87% goes for work amongst those who are already Christians, 12% for work amongst already evangelised non-Christians, and 1% for work amongst people groups who are un-evangelised or unreached. (*Source – article by Randy Alcorn, Giving and The Great Commission, www.epm.org*)

A few observations need to be made from the above statistics:

1. Firstly, according to all available figures, Christian giving to the unreached people groups does not exceed 1% of the total donations received from the Church globally. This is very pathetic! The undeniable fact that

arises from these figures is that completing the Great Commission is definitely not a priority for most churches, Christian leaders, and Believers generally. According to the Scriptures, where our treasure is, there lies our hearts (Matthew 6:21).

2. Secondly, America is by far the most generous giver to world missions. If giving to the unreached people in America averages only 1%, then the Global Church is in a pathetic state.

3. Finally, in view of what we know about the figures of the unreached people groups and the paltry amount that the Global Church channels to them, can we really justify our various expenses on Church buildings, conferences, fat honorariums, hotel expenses and lavish lifestyles that characterise the 21st-century Church?

There are few Christian leaders that have inspired and challenged me more than the late missions statesman Oswald J. Smith, one-time senior Pastor of Peoples Church in Toronto, Canada. In his monumental work – *"The Cry of the World; Marshall Morgan and Scott 1959"*, he presented how his church gave both to home and foreign missions between 1933 and 1963. Without exception, throughout this 30-year period, the church every year gave far more to missions than she spent on the home church. I now present the same giving chart to inspire and challenge the 21-century Christian leaders and Christians generally.

The Peoples Church, Toronto

YEAR	HOME CHURCH ($)	MISSIONS ($)
1933	18,185	23,586
1934	19,822	27,181
1935	26,338	28,102
1937	19,941	30,615
1938	21,230	40,029
1940	22,871	46,435
1941	21,135	54,417
1942	23,144	60,279
1943	23,953	78,413
1944	31,806	117,723
1946	25,379	122,440
1947	28,786	138,394
1948	38,356	177,473
1949	37,215	180,878
1951	38,832	216,443
1952	52,811	228,960
1953	40,813	245,260
1954	39,778	280,423
1956	44,250	289,502
1958	45,549	298,316
1961	49,273	303,345
1963	63,067	329,240

Financial or Discipleship Crisis?

At the moment, a high percentage of Pastors that I interact with are complaining bitterly about an unprecedented decline in church giving, coupled with the fact that traditionally, giving to missionary enterprises, averages an appalling 1% globally. Many believe that there is a financial crisis in the Church. However, I take a different view; I believe what we have on our hands is a discipleship crisis.

There's hardly a better area to test our Christian maturity and commitment than in the area of money. The Bible reveals that Jesus spoke more about money than Heaven. The simple truth is a disciple cannot serve God and money as he will love one and hate the other. Any true disciple will control money, and not the other way round.

One of the best examples of Christian giving can be found among the Macedonian churches and a number of lessons can be learnt from their generosity:

Firstly, they gave themselves completely to the Lord, and then to the Church leaders. This is the secret of acceptable giving to God. When a person is totally given over to the Lord, giving no longer becomes a burden, but a delight.

> *"And this they did, not as we hoped, but first gave their own selves to the Lord and unto us by the will of God." – 2 Corinthians 8:5 (KJV)*

Secondly, their generosity was borne out of a great trial of affliction, and they gave far beyond their means or power. This is a great example for us to follow. We don't only have to give when it is convenient – we can give during our most challenging afflictions; they even gave beyond their power:

> *"How that in a great trial of affliction the abundance of their joy and their deep poverty abounded unto the riches of their liberality. For to their power, I bear record, yea, and beyond their power they were willing of themselves;"* – 2 Corinthians 8:2-3 (KJV)

How Much Shall I Give?

1. If I refuse to give anything to missions this year, I practically cast a ballot in favour of the recall of every missionary.
2. If I give less than heretofore, I favour reduction of the missionary forces proportionate to my reduced contribution.
3. If I give the same as formerly, I favour holding the ground already won, but I oppose any forward movement. My song is "Hold the Forth". All His soldiers are commanded to "Go".
4. If I increase my offering beyond former years, then I favour an advance movement in the conquest of new territory for Christ.

- Quoted from " The Cry of the World – Oswald J. Smith; Marshall Morgan & Scott, page 69, 1959, London"

Practical Application for Finishing the Great Commission

1. In order to finish the Great Commission, the bulk of the Church's finances must be redirected towards the unreached people groups. Do you agree?
2. Financial or discipleship crisis – which one do you think is the most challenging problem confronting the Church today?
3. What lessons can we learn from the chart given of 'the People's Church in Toronto'?
4. Can you determine to begin to give regularly to a missions organisation who is reaching the unreached people groups?

CHAPTER 13

SACRIFICING FOR THE GREAT COMMISSION

"If Jesus Christ be God and died for me, then no sacrifice can be too great for me to make for him" – C.T. Studd

Have you ever wondered why the Church of Christ has been unable to finish the Great Commission after two thousand years? You are definitely not alone! In spite of the fact that no generation of Christians has been materially and financially as prosperous as this generation, about 30% of the 7.5 billion people living today have not heard the name of Jesus Christ once.

In many parts of the world today, born-again Believers are not just among the richest in their nations or regions, but many of them occupy some of the highest political offices in the land. It is very common for

Christian businessmen and women as well as Ministers of the Gospel to own private jets, banks, oil wells, private universities, TV stations, and multinational corporations, to mention these few.

Did you know that according to available statistics, the Church of Christ has over one hundred times the resources needed to plant native churches in all the unreached people groups in the world? I totally agree with John Piper when he declared - *"All the money needed to send and support an army of self-sacrificing joy spreading ambassadors is already in the church."*

The question then is, why have we been unable to finish the Great Commission? To claim that there's only one factor responsible for our inability to take the Gospel to the ends of the earth would be too simplistic. There are definitely a number of reasons that would be attributed to this challenge. However, I am personally convinced that the lack of a sacrificial and simple Christian lifestyle by modern-day Christians is by far one of the key reasons attributed to this delay.

It seems to me that the average Christian today knows little or nothing about a simple and sacrificial lifestyle. Thanks to the prosperity message mostly exported to the world by the church in America.

The Sacrifice Of Christ - Was It Complete?

"Who now rejoice in my sufferings for you, and fill up that which is behind of the afflictions of

> *Christ in my flesh for his body's sake, which is the church"* – *Colossians 1:24 (KJV)*

Let's consider different Bible translations to help us understand the passage better:

> *"And even now I rejoice in the afflictions which I bear for your sake..."* - CON

> *"It is now my happiness to suffer for you..."* – NEB

> *"...And fill up on my part that which is lacking..."* - ASV

> *"...and I'm filling up the things that lack of the tribulations of the Christ in my flesh..."* – RHM

> *"...And in my own person, I supplement the afflictions endured by the Christ..."* – TCNT

In this Bible verse, Paul seems to say that he is filling up or supplementing what is lacking or remaining in the sufferings of Christ. The question which arises now is - when Christ suffered on the Cross and declared that it is finished, what did He mean? Was the suffering necessary for redemption to be complete? If yes, why did Paul still claim to be supplementing the sacrifice or sufferings of Christ?

Again, I don't believe there's any contradiction between what Jesus did and what Paul was claiming. As far as man's redemption is concerned, the price is fully paid for. There is no need for anyone to pay anything to appease God for us to be reconciled to Him. The price has been fully settled once and for all.

However, when it comes to preaching the Gospel and establishing the Saints in the Truth of the Gospel, there's still a price to be paid. This is what Paul was referring to. Anyone who has genuinely been a faithful ambassador of the Good News will tell you the price they have had to pay in order to spread the redemption story. Read Church history, and it is replete with stories of gallant soldiers of the Cross that paid so dearly for others to receive the Gospel.

The Scripture declares regarding the Saints that; "... *they loved not their lives unto death.*" - *Revelation 12:11b (KJV)*

If we are going to advance the Kingdom of God and bring back the King in our generation, we must know something of, and wholeheartedly embrace sacrificial living.

There is a lot Christians need to learn from other religions. Have you considered how many Muslims who belong to organisations such as ISIS and Boko-Haram have paid the ultimate price for the sake of their faith, Islam? I am often put to shame when I read about the sacrifices the apostles and the church fathers paid to give us the Gospel, and how little I know of when it comes to suffering for Christ.

This generation seems to be a sin-loving, pleasure-seeking, God-dishonouring generation. Too many

Christians and Christian leaders are guilty of flamboyant lifestyles, all in the name of living the abundant life.

A Lost Identity

Today's Believers seem to have lost their identity. The blessed Holy Book clearly states what our relationship must be with the world. So, how does the Bible describe us? As pilgrims, strangers or sojourners!

> *"Dearly beloved, I beseech you as strangers and pilgrims, abstain from fleshly lusts, which war against the soul;" – 1 Peter 2:11 (KJV)*

> *"These all died in faith, not having received the promises, but having seen them afar off, and were persuaded of them, and embraced them, and confessed that they were strangers and pilgrims on the earth." – Hebrews 11:13 (KJV)*

Who is a pilgrim or sojourner? This is one who stays in a place or country for a short period. There is a mindset that every pilgrim has; they travel light and are aware that their present abode or station is not their final destination.

I am privileged to have travelled to several nations with the Good News. Once I am in a foreign land, there's a way that I have to conduct myself. For example, I make sure that I travel with essentials which saves me from paying for excess luggage. Also, I do all in my power to obey the laws of my host nation.

As strangers and pilgrims in the world, we are to travel light, as we do not have a permanent residency here on earth; our sojourn is very short. As we have raiment, food and the essentials of life, we must be content!

God promised to supply all our "needs" and not "greed". How many houses, cars, clothes, etc. do we need at any given time? I have lived in England now for over twenty-six years and I have travelled extensively in the western world. One of our most heinous sins, like Sodom, is the fullness of bread.

> *"Behold, this was the iniquity of thy sister Sodom, pride, fullness of bread, and abundance of idleness was in her and in her daughters, neither did she strengthen the hand of the poor and needy." – Ezekiel 16:49 (KJV)*

We waste so many essentials of life; things that we might have given to the less privileged or put into spreading the Good News to foreign lands.

Why are the Labourers Few?

> *"Then saith he unto his disciples, The harvest truly is plenteous, but the labourers are few;" – Matthew 9:37 (KJV)*

Over two thousand years ago, Jesus identified the missionary problem which is the paucity of labourers! The question that confronts us today as Kingdom citizens, chosen by God to depopulate Hell is – "why are Kingdom workers or labourers still few after two thousand years?" Is it because we don't have competent workers? Could it be that the needed knowledge to complete the Great Commission is lacking in the Church? While these reasons might be valid, I am convinced that a high percentage of potential workers are unwilling to sacrifice their present lifestyles, comfort and the cares of this life.

Many will want everything guaranteed before they answer the call. Some today are like the disciples of old who are questioning the Master as to what their reward would be before leaving everything behind and following Him. Jesus' statement is still very true today – "... *when I sent you out without purse, and scrip, and shoes, lacked ye any thing?...*" (Luke 22:35). No one ever serves God faithfully and wholeheartedly who is not rewarded first in this world, and in the world to come.

I remember, very vividly, when I attended Spurgeon's College, London in 1994. I commenced my studies the same month I had my first child, Joshua. I had to pay several thousands for my school fees, without any guaranteed financial support. I also pioneered the World Harvest Christian Centre three months after I started attending the college.

Quite often, I had to study for the Sunday and mid-week service sermons while attending the college. It was very challenging and my classmates, most of whom were sponsored Baptist students, couldn't understand how I could pay such a high price. Well, it's about 25 years now and it's all behind me. If I was to do it again for the sake of Christ and the souls that would be saved, I will not hesitate.

Prosperity Preaching

I once read about a preacher from Africa having a conversation with a missionary from America. He thanked him so much for the contributions of the Church in America, towards the expansion of the Gospel in the world.

Without a doubt, America has sent more missionaries to the nations of the earth - almost more than any other. I'm almost convinced that no other nation has given more money towards missions than America. The world has also benefitted immensely from the ministry gifts of several thousands from the United States.

This African preacher, however, felt that one phenomenon which has not greatly helped the cause of Christ and His Kingdom in Africa was the flavour of the prosperity message brought into Africa. To this, I would unequivocally agree!

I have heard of several "Ministers" of God who would demand that certain amounts of money be transferred into their accounts (often in the hundreds and thousands of dollars) before they accept an invitation to preach the Gospel of Grace. Many would stipulate the kind of hotels, cars, and other things that must be in place in order to "honour" the "anointing" and the "anointed".

Quite often, when these men and women come, the event is nothing more than flesh-mess. Hardly are altar calls made for souls to be saved but several calls are made for all kinds of offerings. We hardly experience the apostolic power being demonstrated in the Acts of the Apostles, yet they make ridiculous demands.

Most Pastors and Church leaders only invite speakers who can pull crowds and raise money and not necessarily people that will challenge the Saints to live a godly life that will please our Saviour.

Do you know how much pressure some Ministers of the Gospel place on their churches in order to drive the latest Jeep? Many ministers will not fly today in economy class, just because they have been "promoted" by God, or they have something to prove to someone.

Please don't get me wrong. There is absolutely nothing wrong in enjoying God's abundant provisions. However, we need to search our hearts and ask ourselves – "is this a need or it's greed?" Could this money be put to better use? Can we really justify having 10 to 15 cars in our garages, when $100 would pay a monthly salary for most missionaries in Africa and Asia?

The Cross

Have you noticed that The Cross is almost a forgotten subject in the Church? You can attend a ministry for several years without hearing a message about The

Cross, and yet The Cross is central to our Faith. It was at The Cross that the sacrifice was paid for our redemption. The Cross stands for denial, sacrifice, death, and the exchanged life.

The central message of the Early Church was The Cross. They not only preached it but quite often, the messenger was in His message.

I believe, when Paul was issuing out a serious warning about false brethren to the Philippian Church, he had the 21st-century also in view.

> *"For many walk, of whom I have told you often, and now tell you even weeping, that they are the enemies of the cross of Christ: Whose end is destruction, whose God is their belly, and whose glory is in their shame, who mind earthly things." – Philippians 3:18-19 (KJV)*

Did you notice how Paul described these false brethren? They were not the enemies of Jesus - but The Cross of Christ.

In order to save the world, God sacrificed His only son. For Abraham to inherit enduring blessings, he had to sacrifice his dear son, Isaac. If we are going to finish the Great Commission in our generation, we must not only rediscover experientially the message of The Cross, but we must begin to live a simple and sacrificial life.

Practical Application for Finishing the Great Commission

1. The absence of the message of the cross on our pulpits today is inadvertently affecting the fortunes of the Great Commission. Do you agree?

2. The prosperity Gospel has done more harm to the cause of Christianity! Comment.

3. Can you list 5 things you can sacrifice in order to be able to support the work of missions?

CHAPTER 14

A CHALLENGE TO THE YOUTH

"Remember now thy Creator in the days of thy youth, while the evil days come not, nor the years draw nigh, when thou shalt say, I have no pleasure in them" - Ecclesiastes 12:1 (KJV)

I am writing this chapter primarily to the youth and to all those who have responsibility for them. They include parents, Bible college presidents, Pastors and church eldership.

So who is a youth? The United Nations, for statistical consistency across regions, defines "youth" as those persons between the ages of 15 and 24 years, without prejudice to other definitions of member states.

Wikipedia defines youth as the time when one is young and often means the time between childhood and adulthood (maturity). It is the period of freshness, vigour and strength.

For the purpose of this book, I would place all those from teenage years to thirty years as youth. The period of one's youth is a very unique stage in life. An understanding of this season and the proper deployment of one's resources and energies would often lead to a fulfilled life.

> *"The glory of young men is their strength..."* - *Proverb 20:29 (KJV)*

> *"Who satisfieth thy mouth with good things; so that thy youth is renewed like the eagle's"* - *Psalm 103:5 (KJV)*

As a young person, your energy level is very high. This is why most sportspersons blossom during their youth! From their thirties, their energy levels begin to dip leading to retirement. Also, young people relatively have more time because more often than not they are not bogged down with the responsibilities of adulthood. In addition, it is characteristic of the youth to take more risks than would an adult. The older we get to, the fewer risks we tend to take.

What does all this tell us? The best time to get serious with God and the Kingdom is in your youthful years. What greater fulfilment can you have in life than in answering the call of God for missions and taking the Gospel to the unreached people? Would you not be greatly satisfied to be the first missionary taking the Gospel of Jesus to a people who have never heard of the glorious Gospel of The Lord?

Biblical evidence reveals to us that most people that God recruits for kingdom work are usually in their youth. Samuel was called as a child and so was Jeremiah. Jesus was thirty years old when he started his public ministry. Moses was called at the age of forty, bearing in mind that this was at a time when life expectancy was much higher than today. Almost all the missionaries that I have studied, answered the call during their youthful stage.

Most of the great Men of God that I know and highly respect started preaching and teaching either in their teenage years or early twenties. By the age of twenty, Charles Spurgeon, the Prince of Preachers, was already Pastoring what would later become one of the biggest churches in Britain. By the age of twenty, I was already preaching in prison, hospitals and our local church.

Dear young person, I encourage you to pray about answering the call for missions, enrolling in a Bible College and preparing yourself for the high call.

Discovering your call and destiny very early in life comes with a lot of benefits; it makes you focused in life. Too many young people waste precious time trying their hands on various unprofitable ventures. I am grateful I discovered my destiny in life at a young age - I knew exactly what I was called to do by the age of 17 and I have stuck to it all these years.

Again, discovering your call into ministry at a young age will help you when making strategic decisions such as your marriage partners. I have always argued that a major recipe for marital bliss is for the couple to discover their God-given destiny before marriage. Many Pastors and Ministers of God who have experienced heartache and marriage break-up have said they would have preferred to have discovered their destiny before choosing a life-partner because many of the people they chose were not ready for ministry.

Practical Application for Finishing the Great Commission

1. Why is it best to answer the call to missions in our youth?
2. Can you name 5 missionaries that answered the call to missions as a youth?
3. As a youth, is it better to discover your calling before making a choice of a life partner?

CHAPTER 15
THE CHURCH PLANTING GOAL

If the 21st-century Church would be serious about completing the Great Commission, we must not just try to secure commitments to Christ; but our goal must be to plant mission-oriented churches!

As great as many evangelistic efforts are, we seem to miss the mark if it doesn't result in the forming of new churches. Church planting, whatever form or shape it takes, is very vital to the evangelisation of the world. Churches are the primary manifestation of God's Kingdom here on earth. It is crucial that I clarify that churches can be expressed differently, that is to say, they may be small or large and may meet in a traditional building or in homes. A church could be made up of professionals, students, children or even retirees. Discipleship and accountability, in my own opinion, is best practised in the context of a church setting.

Several years ago, I came across an interesting book written by the late missiologist Dr. C. Peter Wagner - "Church Planting for Greater Harvest", where he made a remark that has not only inspired but it has propelled me towards greater efforts in church planting. He asserted: *"Church planting is the most effective evangelistic method under Heaven"*. It is argued that every living and healthy thing/being has the potential to reproduce itself! I am a living being and by God's Grace, I have reproduced myself four times. The same applies to churches! Every church is a living organisation and therefore has the potential to reproduce itself within its own culture and beyond. It is for this reason that since we established our ministry over two decades ago, we have endeavoured to plant daughter churches in a number of cities in the United Kingdom and across three other continents of the world.

A classical example of church planting being a tool in finishing the Great Commission can be seen in the church planting initiative of the Redeemed Christian Church of God (RCCG).

The RCCG was founded in 1952 by the late Rev. Josiah Akindayomi in Lagos Nigeria. Pastor Enoch Adejare Adeboye took over the mantle of leadership from the founder in 1981, with just a few branches. However, as of March 2017, the Redeemed Christian Church of God has its presence in 196 countries of the world, with a total membership exceeding 5 million (source –Wikipedia). As of today (2018), it is said that the RCCG has about 42,000 churches in Nigeria. They are by far the largest church in the world today! The only secret has been their aggressive church planting initiative, with the vision of planting churches within 5 minutes of each other.

Writing in the same vein, James Eby, founder and president of Mission Catalyst International, argues that *"In order to finish the Great Commission in this generation, every church should follow Paul's example in Ephesus and the example of the Antioch church in evangelizing its community, province and country by planting other churches."* He further opined:

> *"Everything which is living and healthy grows and reproduces itself. That is true of goats and sheep and camels and trees and flowers and people, etc. These reproductive characteristics should also be true of churches. Healthy churches should always be growing and reproducing by planting other churches in their communities, and by targeting unreached towns and villages which have no church"* James Eby; World Impacting Churches. Tate Publishing; Oklahoma U.S.A. Page 140-141 (2007)

When I was growing up as a boy in the Baptist church in Lagos, I witnessed how the church planted other churches just by starting preaching stations. This to me has been the key to the expansion of the Baptist denomination like other ones.

> *"And when they had preached the gospel to that city, and had taught many, they returned again to Lystra, and to Iconium, and Antioch, Confirming the souls of the disciples, and exhorting them to continue in the faith, and that we must through much tribulation enter into the kingdom of God. And when they had ordained them elders in every church, and had prayed with fasting, they commended them to the Lord, on whom they believed." - Acts 14:21-23 (NKJV)*

Many scholars and Bible commentators have argued from the above Scriptures on the Pauline strategy for church planting. They first preached the Good News (Proclamation); they taught the Word, which is central to discipling, according to the Great Commission mandate. They also helped mature and strengthen the disciples by returning again to the various cities. This is grossly missing today in many evangelistic endeavours. The lack of proper follow-up has been a major bane to most of our outreaches and missionary activities.

In order to have a stable church, Paul ordained elders in every city for these churches. This was meant to help stabilise and strengthen the work when the apostles left.

Finally, they recommended them to the Holy Spirit. Nobody can better keep the work of the ministry more than the Holy Spirit.

"... Not by might, nor by power, but by my Spirit, saith the LORD of hosts." - Zachariah 4:6b (KJV)

It is worth mentioning again that if the 21st-century Church is going to be serious about completing the Great Commission and bringing back our Saviour soon, then the present crop of leaders must be baptised with a fresh vision of church planting - particularly to places where the Gospel is yet to be received.

Practical Application for Finishing the Great Commission

1. To finish the Great Commission, we must plant missions-oriented churches. Do you agree?
2. What would be your top 10 countries that should be our priority in planting churches, in order to finish the Great Commission?
3. Church planters and denominations should target megacities like Paul did when planting churches. Do you agree?

SPECIAL INVITATION

I am totally convinced that this book did not come into your hands by sheer coincidence – it was orchestrated by God!

If you have never at any point in time opened up your heart to receive Jesus and accept Him as your Lord and Personal Saviour – you can do so right now!

Why not say this short prayer?

Dear Jesus! Thank you for dying on the Cross for me. I believe you died and God raised you up on the third day for my salvation. I accept you today as my Lord and Personal Saviour.

Thank you for saving me! Amen!

OTHER TITLES BY THE AUTHOR

If this book has touched you, why not place
an order for other books!

CONTACT DETAILS

World Harvest Christian Centre
7 Enmore Road
South Norwood
London
SE25 5NQ

Tel: + 44 (020) 7358 8080
        + 44 (020) 86545649

Email: admin@worldharvest.org.uk
Website: www.worldharvest.org.uk
Facebook: World Harvest Christian Centre, London
Twitter: @whcc_london, @PastorWale_